BRIDGE
BETWEEN
WORLDS

BOOKS BY DAN MILLMAN

THE PEACEFUL WARRIOR SAGA

Way of the Peaceful Warrior
Sacred Journey of the Peaceful Warrior
The Journeys of Socrates

GUIDEBOOKS

Wisdom of the Peaceful Warrior
Everyday Enlightenment
The Life You Were Born to Live
No Ordinary Moments
The Laws of Spirit
Body Mind Mastery
Living on Purpose

CHILDREN'S BOOKS

Secret of the Peaceful Warrior
Quest for the Crystal Castle

For further information:
www.peacefulwarrior.com

BOOKS BY DOUG CHILDERS

The White-Haired Girl (with Jaia-Sun Childers)
The Energy Prescription (with Connie Grauds)
Minding Your Business (with Horst Rechelbacher)

For further information:
www.dougchilders.com

BRIDGE BETWEEN WORLDS

Extraordinary Experiences
That Changed Lives

DAN MILLMAN
& DOUG CHILDERS

 H J Kramer

published in a joint venture with

 New World Library
Novato, California

An H J Kramer Book
published in a joint venture with
New World Library

Editorial office: Administrative office:
H J Kramer Inc.   New World Library
P.O. Box 1082   14 Pamaron Way
Tiburon, California 94920   Novato, California 94949

Edited by Nancy Carleton
Text design and typography by Tona Pearce Myers
Originally published as *Divine Interventions* in 1999 by Daybreak Books, an imprint of Rodale Books.

Library of Congress Cataloging-in-Publication Data
Millman, Dan.
Bridge between worlds : extraordinary experiences that changed lives / Dan Millman and Doug Childers.
   p.   cm.
Rev. ed. of: Divine interventions.
Includes bibliographical references.
ISBN 978-1-932073-26-3 (pbk. : alk. paper)
1. Miracles—Anecdotes. 2. Providence and government of God—Anecdotes. I. Childers, Douglas. II. Millman, Dan. Divine interventions. III. Title.
BL487.M55 2009
202'.117—dc22   2009036673

First printing, December 2009
ISBN 978-1-932073-26-3
Printed in Canada on 100% postconsumer-waste recycled paper

 New World Library is a proud member of the Green Press Initiative.

10 9 8 7 6 5 4 3 2 1

I had an experience.
I can't prove it . . . I can't even explain it,
but everything that I know as a human being,
everything I am, tells me that it was real.
I was given something wonderful,
something that changed me forever. . . .

—— "DR. ELLIE ARROWAY"
played by Jodie Foster in the film *Contact*

CONTENTS

PREFACE

Bridging Faith and Reason

There are three mysteries in this world:
air to the birds; water to the fish;
and humanity to itself.

—— HILLEL

One night in the summer of 1966, a motorcycle crash shattered the leg and ended the Olympic dreams of a young gymnast named Dan Millman. Twelve years later, on a lonely San Francisco street, two young men clad in black, one armed with a metal pipe, closed in to attack a young writer named Doug Childers.

Back then, Dan and Doug did not know of each other's existence, or that years later their lives would intersect, or that they would become the best of friends. Nor could they perceive a hidden thread that would connect their own turning points to the transformation of other lives.

The experiences related in this book have changed the course of lives and in some cases transformed entire cultures. The value of any experience, whether it seems positive or negative at the time, is best judged not by its drama, but by its fruits. Whether it strikes like lightning or takes root over time, any experience can become a bridge to an unseen reality, a wake-up call that expands awareness, awakens insight, heals wounds, bestows uncommon gifts, unleashes creative abilities, relieves the fear of death, and gives new meaning to life.

Mindfulness teaches us the nature of the shadow;
heartfulness teaches us the nature of the light.
Without these two qualities in balance,
we will evolve either eyeless in the darkness,
or blinded by the light.

— STEPHEN AND ONDREA LEVINE

Within each of us lives a mindful skeptic inclined toward reason, and a heartfelt believer drawn to faith. When asked to choose between these two apparent opposites, the wise embrace both, seeing in each a necessary part of the whole. Only by using the two eyes of faith and reason can we discern the transcendent truths that set us free.

In these pages, we invite believers and skeptics to experience, in their own way, the compelling reports of extraordinary phenomena that changed lives. Some of the events we describe appear to transcend or suspend the laws of physics. Do such stories truly demonstrate miraculous phenomena? Or do they simply reflect unknown laws, yet to be discovered?

Our universe may contain many realities, each one operating according to its own internal laws. Our body/minds may contain built-in mechanisms and inherent yet latent capacities we don't fully understand that account for spontaneous healings, visionary experiences, and extraordinary abilities. What we call the supernatural may be quite natural after all.

Some of the most "unbelievable" stories in this book are also the most well documented. But in the end, doubts about the reality of the phenomena described are balanced by the compelling evidence of lives transformed. Must an apparition appear in an outward or tangible form to be "real"? How substantial is light? How tangible is love? Are angels who appear only in our visions less than real if they transform our hearts and minds and change the course of our lives?

Like all true mysteries, the stories in this book yield no final answers to life's larger questions. But they may inspire hope and reawaken a sense of reverence, wonder, and awe. They may remind us of our innate potential, and of a mysterious power that lives in each of us, as close as our heartbeat, as this present moment, as our next breath.

In our research and selection process, we declined obvious fiction or fantasy as well as events easily explained away as coincidence, suggestion, or wishful thinking. We checked and cross-referenced a variety of sources to establish, as much as possible, the validity of the events and phenomena described. Even historical records are based on subjective perceptions, partial descriptions, hearsay, and memory, and leave out innumerable relevant factors. No story, no history, no belief, is unquestionably true. It is not our business or mission to impose on readers a particular spiritual worldview. We let the stories speak for themselves.

Of course, sometimes the stories may provoke us to ask why one person is saved from peril while others are lost; why evil seems at times to triumph over good; why some are miraculously healed of affliction or reborn in spirit through adversity, while others die of their diseases or succumb to despair.

Perhaps the challenge for each of us is to find meaning in our own suffering, and a spiritual purpose in our own adversity. Perhaps the inescapable difficulties and disappointments of life, and the journeys through darkness and light, are essential for our spiritual education and evolution. Take a moment to consider your own life — are you stronger, wiser, and more compassionate as a result of your struggles and your suffering?

Ultimately, life unfolds as it will, beyond our control and understanding. We may desire healing, but we cannot dictate its appearance or, if it comes, what form it will take. Hoped-for physical regeneration may fail, even as deeper emotional wounds are healed and our spirits are awakened. Unwelcome, unexpected pain may be the perfect catalyst that reveals to us our own true nature and serves our ultimate destiny. We cannot always know or predict what our highest good requires. And rarely do we notice the transcendental perfection of this evolving, at times troubled world.

Taken together, these stories remind us that we live in a more mysterious, and perhaps more perfect, universe than we usually notice; that unexplored territory remains hidden behind the seemingly mundane surface of our daily lives and in the depths of our own psyches; and that undreamed-of possibilities may wait for us on the other side of the bridge between worlds.

So join us now for a mystery tour through a living portrait gallery highlighting humanity's contact with a timeless power, appearing in many forms, that continues to stir our imaginations and awaken our souls — a power that flows through and nourishes all living things, that makes saints of schoolgirls and sages of kings, and turns everyday life into the most extraordinary adventure of all.

DAN MILLMAN

DOUG CHILDERS

One cannot help but be in awe,
contemplating the marvelous structure of reality.
It is enough if one tries merely to comprehend
a little of this mystery every day.

— ALBERT EINSTEIN

One of the reasons religion seems irrelevant today
is that many of us no longer have the sense
that we are surrounded by the unseen.

— KAREN ARMSTRONG, *A History of God*

A single event can awaken within us
a stranger previously unknown to us.

— ANTOINE DE SAINT EXUPÉRY

CITIZEN OF THE UNIVERSE

The Transformation of Bucky Fuller

Until he was four years old, little cross-eyed Bucky Fuller saw the world as a blur of shapes and colors; he didn't even know what the members of his own family looked like. When he got his first pair of glasses, the sight of the world struck him with the force of a revelation. "For the first time," he said, "I saw leaves on a tree, small birds . . . the stars and the shapes of clouds and people's faces. It was a time of utter joy, as though all these things had been newly created just for me. I was filled with wonder at the beauty of the world."

When Bucky was thirteen, his father died after a series of strokes. The resulting family crises catapulted him out of the magical realm of childhood into a harsher, more troubled world in which he often felt awkward and isolated.

Years later, through family connections, Bucky was accepted into Harvard University, where his quirky personality made him an outsider; a sense of alienation tormented this sensitive youth and brought out his reckless side. That first year, as midterm approached, Bucky impulsively withdrew the funds his mother had saved for his education, went to New York City, lodged in one of its finest hotels, and attended the Ziegfeld Follies. Captivated by the show's star, he returned the next night, sent roses and five bottles of champagne backstage, and, in a grand self-destructive gesture, took the entire cast out for a party at one of New York's finest restaurants. In one evening he squandered his entire college fund and ran up a bill it would take his family years to pay.

In the aftermath, Harvard expelled Bucky for irresponsible conduct and his mother sent him to work as an apprentice mechanic in a Connecticut textile mill. A blessing in disguise, this stimulated in Bucky a natural aptitude for mechanical engineering. He threw himself into his work with a passion, sketching his ideas and designing new mechanical pieces for textile machinery. He received glowing work reports and was eventually allowed to return home, rehabilitated in his family's eyes.

At twenty, Bucky met Anne Hewlett, the young woman he would marry in 1917 and love until the day he died. When World War I began, he joined the Navy and patrolled the New England coast searching for German U-boats. Though still a bit odd and erratic, Bucky was a bright, likable young man with a zest for life and a creative knack for inventing "contraptions."

When the war ended, Bucky returned home to his beloved Anne and their infant daughter, Alexandra. By that time Alexandra had suffered bouts of polio and spinal meningitis that left her partially paralyzed. To help cover the extra expenses, Bucky found a high-paying job. But three months after he had begun, the company shut down, leaving him penniless and unable to find decent work. Everything seemed to go wrong after that. At twenty-seven Bucky began to look and feel like a failure. He'd never been a drinker, but now he became one.

In the midst of this difficult period, to distract himself from a chronic depression, Bucky decided to attend a Yale-Harvard football game with some old college chums. Before leaving home, Bucky, Anne, and Alexandra took a walk in the fresh air. Seeing her father's cane, which he used due to an old knee injury, Alexandra asked, "Daddy, when you come home, will you bring me a cane?" He promised he would.

To Bucky's delight, Harvard won the game, and he spent the night drinking and celebrating. The next day he phoned home from Pennsylvania Station to find Anne distraught. Their beloved Alexandra had caught pneumonia and now lay in a coma. She was still unconscious when Bucky arrived. She awoke only once, looked up at him, and asked, "Daddy, did you bring me my cane?"

Bucky turned away in agony and shame, unable to meet his daughter's eyes — he'd forgotten all about his promise. Alexandra died that night in his arms.

Forty years later, Bucky still couldn't speak of this incident without weeping. It would haunt him for the rest of his life. Bucky was devastated, driven nearly out of his mind with guilt and grief, and stricken by his loss, his inability to provide for his family, his self-centered nature, and his failures.

That same season, Anne's mother, one of her brothers, and her brother-in-law also died. Bucky called it "a winter of horror." To escape his personal and financial abyss, he started a company designing and building construction machinery. Each day after work he came home and drank long into the night.

After five difficult years, with the nation moving toward the Great Depression of the 1930s, Bucky and Anne had another daughter, named Alegra. Bucky's struggling company was bought out by a large corporation; he became an employee, and was fired. Once again, he became a pauper with a wife and newborn child to support. These blows destroyed his last shred of faith in himself. Believing he was cursed — and fated to bring tragedy and suffering to those he loved — he fell into a suicidal depression.

On a bitterly cold winter evening, in a mood of utter despair, thirty-four-year-old Bucky Fuller walked out of his apartment down to the shores of Lake Michigan, determined to throw himself into the frigid waters. "I've done the best I know how and it hasn't worked," he declared to himself. "I'm just no good." His own mother had believed he might turn out worthless, and had told him so — she had even tried to stop his wedding, warning her future in-laws that he was too irresponsible to support a family. Now, it seemed, she was right about everything.

As Bucky stood on the windy shores of Lake Michigan, his mind suddenly cleared, and he began a sober and spontaneous inquiry into his life, its worth and purpose, and the ultimate origins of his being. He determined then and there to discover the truth about himself, and then to act upon what he found — to live or die. If he was worthless, a "bad man" as some said, destructive to those he loved, he would end his life in the freezing waters. Anne would find someone better, Alegra was too young to miss him, and his in-laws could easily support them both if he were gone, or so he reasoned.

With a sudden urgency, questions arose in him: Was there a divine intelligence in the universe? Was his life of any value? Bucky resolved to accept only the evidence of his own perceptions, not what he'd learned or been told by others. As his intense questioning deepened and as he considered the nature of reality, he experienced a sudden and overwhelming inner certainty that a divine intelligence existed. His engineer's vision saw proof of this not in beliefs or dogmas, but in the universe itself — in "the exquisite design of everything from the invisible microcosm of atoms to the macro-magnitudes of the galaxies, and all of them inter-accommodating with absolute integrity."

Next, Bucky began a heartfelt inquiry concerning whether he might "be of any value to the integrity of Universe." As Bucky reviewed his whole life and all he'd learned, an intelligent pattern began to emerge. And in a moment of supreme insight, he knew: "You do not have the right to eliminate yourself; you do not belong to you. You belong to the universe. Your significance will remain forever obscure to you, but you may assume that you are fulfilling your role if you apply yourself to converting your experience to the highest advantage of others."

These insights struck Bucky with the force of a command — as if his soul had perched on his shoulder and counseled his mortal self. That night Bucky Fuller went home a changed man. With a profound new sense of inner strength and purpose, he knew that to go on living he was called to consecrate himself to the highest purpose of serving others and his world, of working "for the total well-being of people everywhere."

Bucky knew he had no gift for reforming humanity; rather, his abilities were uniquely suited for reforming the environment. He decided he would no longer worry about money. "If the Intelligence directing Universe really has a use for me, it will not allow us to starve; it will see to it that I am able to carry out my resolve."

Within a matter of hours, a new vision of his life's purpose had unfolded in Bucky's mind; an inner revelation had completely reorganized his being. The only thing remaining was to act. He returned to Anne and told her what had occurred, and how he intended to live. And this remarkable woman not only understood his vision, but also agreed to his purpose. The radical nature of

Bucky's transformation revealed itself in the way he went about changing his life, deepening his illumination begun on the shores of Lake Michigan. Determined to unlearn the mass of secondhand beliefs and opinions that filtered and distorted his direct perceptions, he now rarely spoke, and then only to convey essential communications to Anne and Alegra.

Anne became his voice to the outside world.

Driven by a profound urgency, Bucky moved his family to a cheap apartment in a poor section of Chicago and dedicated himself to prolonged contemplation and rigorous study, hoping to discover "the wellspring of true creativity and authentic life, to regain the sensitivities I was born with." To salvage every possible moment, Bucky began napping briefly when his mind began to flag, in time cutting his sleep to two or three hours out of twenty-four. His friends and family thought his behavior wildly irresponsible, perhaps insane. Anne alone understood and stood by him, picking up the slack and defending him to the world.

As it turned out, Bucky's peculiar experiment released tremendous reserves of energy and creativity in him. Alden Hatch, his biographer and friend of many decades, wrote: "From this intense period of silent thought emerged in embryo most of the great philosophical and mathematical innovations that have made his fame and moved the world forward."

Remarkable ideas, insights, and information began to pour through Bucky, among them his radical architectural innovations. The solar-powered house-on-a-pole, his first famous invention, recycled all water and wastes or turned them into fertilizer. It weighed six thousand pounds and cost fifteen hundred dollars.

In 1929 Bucky broke his silence; his friends joked that he never stopped talking again. In fact, he became a prolific lecturer and writer to explain his revolutionary ideas and inventions. He de-signed a car that traveled on land and water, and also flew. This aerodynamic Dymaxion car, with a land speed of 120 mph, was twenty years ahead of its time. When his circular Dymaxion house was shown to the public, thirty thousand orders flooded in.

But Bucky's most successful architectural design, for which he would become known worldwide, was the geodesic dome — the simplest, most durable, economical, and elegant architectural struc-ture ever devised. It could be assembled in hours and withstand winds up to two hundred miles per hour. The U.S. Marines pur-chased over three hundred domes. The Air Force used them as Antarctic bases. His famed aluminum-skinned Kaiser Dome musi-cal auditorium in Honolulu, roughly fifty yards in diameter, was constructed in only twenty-two hours.

Bucky also designed a self-contained, solar-powered pyrami-dal city of the future that floated on the sea. His lightweight trans-parent domes could cover conventional cities and create perfect atmospheres. A pioneer global visionary, Bucky saw humanity as a crew of astronauts soaring through the galaxy on Spaceship Earth — citizens not of nations but of the universe itself.

Of course, Bucky was now able to afford a far more comfort-able home and neighborhood for Anne and Alegra. Anne remained the one constant throughout his long, creative whirlwind life. Now certain of immortality beyond bodily death, Bucky made Anne this promise: He would die before her so that he could greet her on the other side.

One day, after lecturing in New York City, Bucky, then in his eighties, got a telephone call. Anne, back in Los Angeles, was in the hospital, seriously ill. He caught the first plane back, but by the time he arrived Anne had lapsed into a coma. The doctors doubted she would regain consciousness. Once again Bucky had returned too late. Perhaps Bucky recalled the heartrending incident decades earlier — his forgotten promise to buy his dying daughter Alexandra a cane.

Bucky set a chair by Anne's bed as she lay unconscious, her breathing faint. He spoke to her softly for a few moments. Then Bucky Fuller leaned back, closed his eyes, and quietly died. Minutes later, a nurse came in and found him. Bucky had kept his promise. Anne, the love of his life, followed him several hours later.

Perhaps Alexandra was there to greet them both on the other side, waiting just across the bridge between worlds.

SURRENDER IN THE FLAMES

A Gift from the Inferno

The night before the house burned down with Valerie Vener inside it, she and her college roommate had sat on the front porch discussing the worst way to die. Her roommate feared drowning; Valerie's worst-case scenario was death by fire.

The following evening, the full moon of July 15, 1981, both Valerie and her roommate were invited to a party. At the last minute, Valerie, who was exhausted, went to bed at eight o'clock and fell deeply asleep. The fire department later determined that the blaze started at about 9:30 PM directly below her, in a living room uniquely insulated by plush furniture, Persian carpets, and two walls lined floor to ceiling with record albums.

The fire smoldered for half an hour in the contained environment, heating the room like a kiln, melting the records and unleashing thick, black, toxic smoke. As fire spread across the lower floor, poisonous fumes permeated the house and rose to fill the entire upper floor, including the room where Valerie was sleeping. At approximately 10:15 PM, a stifling heat and hellish stench awakened her. She sat upright in bed in an eerie darkness, woozy from oxygen deprivation and the heat, drugged by the toxic fumes she'd been breathing for half an hour. The light shining into her room illumined an ethereal realm of smoky vapor. As she later recalled:

I was in a dreamlike state. Time had stopped. I felt both crystal clear and utterly disoriented. The environment was so bizarre. The usual laws of physics no longer seemed to apply. Logically, I should have panicked from the stench, abnormal heat, and darkness. But all I could imagine was that one of my roommates had left a pot burning on the stove.

Valerie started for the bedroom door to call downstairs, but stopped in her tracks when she spied several large, oval-shaped forms made of smoke hovering nearby. They appeared as pulsing, living beings — their outer structures enclosing a kind of circulatory system made of swirling smoke, Mobius-like threads spiraling up and down inside them like internal energy circuitry. "Their beauty was mesmerizing," Valerie recalled. She stopped before one of them and gazed in awe, not yet wondering what the smoke was doing in her room, until the overwhelming stench and the pain of breathing brought her back to a momentary sense of reality.

Valerie pushed at the door, already several inches ajar. It seemed heavy, as if some outside force resisted. Peering into the hall she saw only impenetrable darkness. For the first time, fear pierced her dreamlike state. She did not yet realize the house was on fire — only that something was terribly wrong. She stepped into a hallway so dark she couldn't even see her hands, instinctively raised to protect her face from the extreme heat. Now she noticed a muffled, rumbling roar below, like a distant train.

Valerie found her way down the hall to the stairs, where another wall stopped her with tangible force. It was a blast of searing heat, sucked up the stairs by an open window acting as a chimney. The first floor was now engulfed in flames. (The fire report later determined that temperatures in the house ranged from 1200 to 1700 degrees Fahrenheit).

In toxic shock, Valerie's mind clung to the idea of a burning pot on the stove. She tried calling out with a rasping croak. But with each breath she took, the repulsive stench and infernal heat blistered her nose and throat. Then, out of the darkness at the top of the stairs, a huge tongue of fire darted out at her, shocking her awake. Suddenly, everything was obvious. In terror, Valerie groped for the hall phone, lifted the receiver and dialed zero.

"Operator," came the answer.

"I'm at five twenty-four South Forest Avenue!" Valerie gasped. "Five twenty-four South Forest Avenue! On the corner of University! My house is on fire! I'm in the house! It's five twenty-four South Forest Avenue!"

"Ma'am, I'm sorry; I'll put you on hold for a moment."

Valerie dropped the phone. She didn't know she was being connected to the fire department, only that her house was burning down and she was being put on hold. She ran into her room, thinking she'd climb out her window. If she hung from the sill by her fingers before letting go, it might be a twenty-foot drop to the street. With her years of professional dance training and her two-mile daily swims, she felt she could survive the fall without serious injury. Anything was better than burning.

Valerie reached the window, but as she tried to remove the screen, the window cracked and broke. Instantly, with a stunning power and finality, a wall of fire roared up from below, inches from her face, blocking her escape. She was in the fire's domain, under its absolute authority.

Now Valerie made out voices from the street below, shouting, laughing, talking excitedly. Trapped in her room by a wall of fire, Valerie listened as the sound of human voices beyond her reach increased her feelings of helplessness and isolation. Then she heard a shout from inside the house: "Valerie! Come downstairs! Follow my voice! Follow my voice!" She ran down the hall to the stairs, took one step down, and reeled back as a force field of rising heat singed her brows and lashes and burned several inches off of her hair.

"Get out!" she heard a woman scream. "The walls are caving in! Get out!"

"No!" a man shouted. "I can get her! She's upstairs!"

"Get out! Get out now!" the woman shrieked.

Then the walls and floor began to shake, and the voices stopped.

Valerie was trapped, and no one was coming to get her. Turning around, she saw flames darting from under the doors of the other two bedrooms. She stumbled back and stood in her doorway, looking into her room at the fire, which seemed to have a malevolent presence. She watched her plants shrivel and die in seconds, their life force consumed by the heat.

Blossoms of flame burst forth in spontaneous combustion, devouring the curtains, darting as if with intention across the room, leaping over her bed to engulf the writings and poetry she had stored under a bookshelf, igniting her paintings and burning them off the walls.

"The fire consumed my personal treasures one by one," Valerie recalled. "My life was being sacrificed before my very eyes." The house, now a furnace, shook and roared. Valerie struggled to breathe as the fire consumed the remaining oxygen. Heat seared her lungs. The room was ablaze now as orange tongues of flame licked along the walls and ceiling, darted from under the doors, and closed in on her from all directions. There was no way out. She could not be saved.

Valerie knew she was going to die.

Valerie later recalled:

In a moment, all the fear — the anguish of isolation and abandonment, the horror of dying — rose to an unbearable pitch. I realized that these core emotions had always been ever-present forces in my life — forces that I had, until now, been afraid to allow. In this extraordinary moment, I had no choice but to surrender completely to my inevitable death.

With this surrender came an instantaneous change of perception. Suddenly I had never seen anything more beautiful than the inside of a fire. Even the sounds were enchanting — the flames were dancing, thundering, and fluttering at the tops like thousands of bird wings. The fire had a wondrous presence. It seemed amusing that I could have been so terrified of such an exquisite phenomenon. Nothing had changed except my point of view, as a direct result of my surrender.

Valerie, absorbed in this beauty, found herself looking down with detachment at her body lying crumpled outside the doorway. Quite naturally, she continued to surrender, and her awareness continued to expand. She saw a large crowd of people and many fire trucks arriving outside; she passed through a realm of gold, then into a marvelous and blissful blue, and finally into an indescribable realm of white radiance.

Minutes later the firefighters made it upstairs, after their hoses cooled down the house. They found Valerie in the smoke-darkened hall and carried her outside. She had no pulse or breath. Of the three paramedics who tried to revive her, two finally pronounced her dead of smoke inhalation. In the white light, Valerie knew nothing of the drama going on around her lifeless body:

> *This radiance, so absolutely brilliant, left nothing to be desired. There was nothing to reach for, no dilemma at all. I knew this white light is what we try to describe in human terms as "God." It was also my core self. I saw with humor and compassion how "Valerie" — the one who was identified with the body I had left behind — desired to "do good," to control life, to survive. It was now obvious that "Valerie" was never in control, could never be in control, and that the fear that drove the desire to control was absolutely unnecessary.*

Then a bright entity of golden white light appeared, emanating absolute love. This being seemed more expanded than, yet not separate from, herself. Valerie internally heard his perfect communication: "You were frightened, eh?" They laughed together at the joke of it all. Her surrender had only brought her closer to herself, a return to her origins in this radiance. In the end this being gave her two choices: to return to her present body, or to take on a new one. "Either way he said I was his — that I would always be his, and that he loved me. No ownership was implied in his words. Only perfect, eternal love."

Meanwhile Valerie's body lay on the front yard. Although she had been pronounced dead, the third paramedic refused to give up his efforts at resuscitation. He felt certain that she was *supposed* to live. He persisted alone for several minutes. Valerie's heart began beating again.

Valerie violently awakened in an ambulance on the way to the hospital, in searing pain, her body blackened by toxic smoke. Incredibly, she had fallen in the only area and physical position in which she could have survived until the firefighters found her, with a carpet somehow wrapped around her vital parts.

In her forty-five-minute ordeal, nine pounds were cooked from her body. Her survival and full recovery, with minimal burns (mostly on her arms), and her lack of brain damage from the oxygen deprivation and toxic smoke inhalation, were called miraculous.

Valerie's experience, her trust in the power of surrender, and her new sense of self helped her get through the prolonged ordeal of recovery. Her struggle to remember and maintain her hard-earned wisdom in the face of severe emotional and physical pain helped her develop the ability to accept and embrace life even in its most difficult moments. She became attracted to meditation and other disciplines of attention that drew her back to the tacit memory of freedom experienced in the flames.

Valerie Vener went on to teach others the spiritual lessons of surrender she learned in the fire, and in the light.

BROTHERS AFTER ALL

A Moment of Grace in the Moment of Truth

D oug Childers was born in rural Kentucky in the summer of
1956. His family rarely stayed in one place for more than two
years, and by age twelve he had moved eight times to eight different states. In 1968, during the height of the antiwar protests over
Vietnam, Doug's family moved to Grand Forks, North Dakota, a
farming town with a university and a military base.

Tensions ran high between the local military families and
the student protesters, whom Doug resembled only by virtue of
his long hair. This was enough to arouse the animosity of his
teachers and his junior high school peers. When a number of the
tougher students began a campaign of physical harassment to force
Doug to cut his hair, he refused to back down. As a result, for the
next three years, he endured pain and humiliation in the form of
frequent physical assaults by groups of local toughs both in and
out of school.

For years after, Doug lived on alert, with a clenching fear and
a burning anger. Then, at the age of twenty, he began studying the
martial arts. In his third year of intensive training, realizing he could
now skillfully defend himself, he experienced an exhilarating sense

of freedom. His fear of assault vanished, resulting in a reckless confidence. On a number of occasions he roamed through San Francisco's notorious Tenderloin district in the middle of the night, enjoying a sense of liberation in one of the city's most dangerous, crime-ridden neighborhoods.

He never even considered that he might be tempting fate.

Meanwhile, his buried anger manifested in an endless stream of martial art fantasies — mental rehearsals in which Doug visualized attacks like those he had suffered in earlier years, now met with his newly cultivated fighting skills. Although philosophically disposed to pacifism, Doug knew that a part of him secretly wanted a real-life payback against "the bad guys" for his years as a victim of violence.

Then, in 1978, while walking home from a friend's at 3:00 AM one chilly San Francisco morning, Doug rounded the corner onto his street and saw two young men about thirty yards ahead, dressed in black from their shoes to their knit wool caps. He felt a sudden chill at the sound of a high-pitched *ping* as one of them tapped a foot-long metal pipe against a brick building.

"Okay, guys," he whispered, "just walk past my house and let me go inside." One of the men glanced back, saw Doug, and nudged his friend. Now they both looked back and began calling out taunting, threatening words. Doug felt a surge of adrenaline, and kept walking; just as he had refused to cut his hair years ago under threats and violence, he now refused to flee from his own house.

The two men stopped in the next doorway to wait for him.

As he approached the two men, Doug's body felt electrified and his mind was uncommonly lucid. He felt certain he could handle the situation: They were two to his one, but clearly overconfident; he was harmless looking, trained to fight multiple opponents, and had the element of surprise. With his senses heightened, Doug prepared for a fight he expected to last a few seconds, and for a payback years delayed.

As he drew near, Doug took note of their positions, visualizing how they would come for him, and what he would do: They would come out of the doorway; he'd throw his keys in the face of the one with the pipe and deliver the sudden foot and hand strikes to stomach and head that he'd practiced for years. In his mind's eye he saw them fall to the sidewalk, writhing in pain, mouths and noses bleeding from ruptured internal organs.

But in an instant, Doug experienced a radical reversal in consciousness that would change his life forever. The realization struck him that he had the power to injure these strangers, but not the power to heal them. And a profound revulsion overwhelmed him — a sense of grief and remorse over what he was about to do. Suddenly the scenario he had imagined, and was perhaps about to occur, made no sense.

Doug describes what happened next:

I now approached them with a kind of bemused bewilderment. My mind had shifted to an expanded perspective from which our little drama seemed utterly ludicrous. We three fools stood there among billions of people on earth, trapped in a silly game. It was obvious to me that we had no idea why we were doing this, or even how we got on this planet. We'd never met, yet we were about to engage in mortal combat as if we were enemies. It was absurd! I felt a profound, exhilarating sense of brotherhood, even affection, for these two men. My fear and all plans of attack simply vanished. I didn't decide not to fight — the possibility disappeared from my mind in a kind of divine amnesia I can't explain to this day. I felt no fear, no sense of danger — only an absolute, joyous certainty that I loved these men as brothers.

This view was not a strategy or philosophy, but a realization. Doug, a trained fighter with no religious background or experience, didn't believe that love conquered all or that thinking positive thoughts could resolve a violent confrontation. In his usual frame of mind, this behavior would have been unrealistic and dangerous. But Doug was not in his usual frame of mind.

The two men stepped out of the doorway toward him, one with the pipe raised just as Doug had visualized. Doug grinned at them as if greeting long-lost friends. In his profoundly altered state, it never even occurred to him that he was in any danger — that these men, his brothers, might harm him. "I was overjoyed to see them," he recalled. With a huge smile, he looked into the eyes of a young black man about his age, and said in a loud, affectionate voice, "Hey! How are you?" The man froze like a statue with his pipe in the air. Doug then smiled at his young Hispanic friend and said, "Good evening!"

Both young men stood looking at Doug with dumbstruck faces:

I think they felt that I loved them, and they didn't know what to do; they'd been short-circuited. I walked on — it felt like floating — two houses past them to my front door, in no hurry at all. I went inside and stood in the dark. I was flooded with ecstasy, surrounded by a marvelous presence. In an inner vision, I saw and felt with utter clarity the world bathed in light — it was absolutely alive, divinely perfect. I knew all human beings were my brothers and sisters. I loved the whole world and everyone in it. As I basked in this remarkable state, I heard the two men run off down the street.

In the days and weeks that followed, Doug pondered this experience. What had transpired was far beyond an expansive mood or a lucky break. The event had changed him. Formerly an atheistic skeptic, Doug now experienced a profound curiosity about the nature of reality. In time it evolved into a spiritual search to which he would devote many years.

As Doug put it:

That event taught me there is always a higher solution to any difficulty. When things get difficult, I look for that higher road. I also learned that a mysterious presence and power that can radically alter our consciousness and facilitate extraordinary life changes is available to anyone who sincerely opens to it. Finally, I came to understand that the greatest power we have in life is our ability to make simple, loving contact with other human beings.

Meeting hatred with love is one of the highest and most difficult practices of life. Doug would have been justified in defending himself, and might have defeated them in battle, settling an old childhood score.

Instead, he realized that they were brothers after all.

MYSTERIES OF HEAVEN AND HELL

Science's Magnificent Mystic

For many of us, the word *mystic* conjures up images of impractical, otherworldly souls with their heads in the clouds and their feet who knows where. But the early life of Emanuel Swedenborg reveals an eminently rational man, a renowned technical innovator, and a scientific genius — an unlikely candidate for the legendary mystic he was to become.

In his home country of Sweden, Emanuel was a respected renaissance man. Among his many positions, he served as the king's appointed royal scientist, and a member of the Swedish House of Nobles, where he wrote legislative bills in areas of national interest. Fluent in nine languages, he wrote primarily in Latin, the scholarly language of his day. In his spare time, he learned to bind books and to make watches, cabinets, and scientific instruments. Also an astronomer, medical scientist, and mechanical engineer, Emanuel ground the lenses to build his own telescope and microscope. He designed, among other things, an air gun, a submarine (never built), an airplane (built and flown two centuries later in the early 1900s), a music machine, a house heater, and a fire extinguisher. He also designed the world's largest dry dock; then, for

the king of Sweden, Emanuel supervised the transport of a fleet of
ships fourteen miles over the mountains, resulting in a crucial military victory.

When applied to Emanuel, the terms *brilliant* and *practical* are
understatements: By 1742, at the age of fifty-six, he had mastered
all known branches of science and developed several new ones.
He had written 150 works, summarizing the discoveries and knowledge in each of these varied fields and gathering their data into
coherent systems (often making his own new discoveries along the
way) before moving on to the next field. And after Emanuel de-
voured and recapitulated all the human knowledge of his era, he
decided to prove the existence of the soul.

In the process he became a mystic.

After completing his exploration of the territory of the outer
world, it was only natural for Emanuel to turn his seemingly infinite intellect to the inner world. As a scientist, he knew he would
need to look inward to discover the soul. So he began to analyze
his dreams, and to explore his own mind through a direct and
deliberate meditative process. Along the way he encountered ele-
ments of his "shadow side" — his arrogance and the "impurity of
soul." (In fact, his insightful writings foreshadow the future science
of psychology; psychiatrist Carl Jung would later owe Emanuel
Swedenborg a great debt.)

As it happened, Emanuel's inner explorations initiated a profound and at times violent process of purification that finally gave
way to surrender, and to a genuine humility before a divine presence that would help him on his quest. In his writings he described
one such event:

> *Immediately there came over me a powerful tremor ... together*
> *with a resounding noise like great winds clashing. I found that*

something holy had encompassed me . . . it shook me and pros-
trated me on my face. I saw that I was thrown down and I
found the words put into my mouth, "Oh, thou almighty Jesus
Christ, who of thy great mercy deignest to come to so great a
sinner, make me worthy of this grace!" I prayed and there
came forth a hand that pressed my hands. . . . I was sitting at
His bosom and beheld Him face to face . . . a countenance of
such holy mien that cannot be expressed.

It seemed Christ spoke to him, saying, "Love me truly," or
"Do what thou hast promised."

Such blessed chastisements profoundly moved the stately
scientist, transforming him, for all his remaining years, into a
humble, even childlike man of faith. He came to understand that
the intellect of which he was so proud couldn't of itself produce
everlasting truth, wisdom, or peace. These qualities, Emanuel
now realized, existed eternally, prior to the mind, and came only
from God.

A singular vision had initiated Emanuel Swedenborg's mystical journey. The spiritual seeds germinated within him, in time
bringing profound revelations and insights. And a door to other
worlds would soon open before him.

One night an apparently human figure suddenly appeared to
him in his room:

He said that he was the Lord God, the Creator of the world,
and the Redeemer, and that he had chosen me to explain to
men the spiritual sense of the Scripture, and that He Himself
would explain to me what I should write on this subject. That
same night were opened to me, so that I became thoroughly
convinced of their reality, the worlds of spirits, heaven and
hell. I recognized there, many acquaintances of every condition

in life. From that day I gave up the study of all worldly science and devoted my labors to spiritual things, accordingly as the Lord had commanded me to write. Afterwards the Lord opened daily and often my bodily eyes, so that I could see into the other world, and in a state of perfect wakefulness, converse with angels and spirits.

This appears to be the testimony either of an extraordinary mystic or a raving madman. Yet Emanuel's whole life before this event was one of supreme ability and sanity. And the quality of his accomplishments and writings that followed also judge the matter in his favor.

Over the next thirty years Swedenborg produced thirty-six volumes; in them he wrote in meticulous detail about various heavens and hells; about the nature of God, angels, and demons; about humanity's relationship with all the above; about what happens to us after death; and more.

Emanuel's inner life bore the fruit of mysterious powers reported by many credible witnesses. Once Queen Louisa asked Swedenborg to contact her recently deceased brother. Days later he delivered an intimate message to the queen from her brother that so shocked her she left the court immediately, pale and shaking. She later reported that Swedenborg had given her information that no living person could have known.

On July 17, 1759, Swedenborg attended a large dinner party in Gothenburg at the house of a wealthy merchant, William Castel. At six o'clock, Swedenborg became extremely agitated. Asked what the matter was, he described in detail a fire burning three hundred miles away in the city of Stockholm.

News of Swedenborg's report spread through the town. When the governor heard the story, he summoned Emanuel to his home for a detailed report of the fire. Swedenborg told him where, when, and how it started — even which houses were burned. Two days later when messengers arrived from Stockholm, Swedenborg's report proved accurate in every detail.

At another party — as it happened, the very night Emperor Peter III of Russia was strangled in prison — Swedenborg became agitated and went into a trance. When he came to, the guests insisted he tell what he had seen. With great emotion, he described in vivid detail the death of the Russian emperor, asking the guests to note the time and date so as to compare it when reports arrived. Days later, Russian newspaper reports matched Swedenborg's vision.

At times, Swedenborg's humor had a moral edge. Declaring the futility of outward displays of piety, he taught that only charitable service ultimately mattered. He once attended a party with Archbishop Troilus, a passionate gambler in a card game called Tresett, whose gambling partner, Erland Broman, had recently died. "Tell us about the spirit world," the archbishop taunted Swedenborg. "How does my friend Broman spend his time there?"

"I saw him but a few hours ago shuffling his cards in the company of the Evil One," retorted Swedenborg. "And he was only waiting for Your Worship to make up a game of Tresett."

Emanuel Swedenborg wrote that angels and demons exist in their own realms, and also within our minds — that our thoughts, feelings, and impulses emanate from these inner residents. We live, he wrote, in a space of free will between heaven and hell; our spiritual challenge is to choose the good in any moment amidst the tumult of these forces within us.

Swendenborg saw the soul defined by choices and acts, not beliefs or professed ideals. He stated that the soul chose heaven or hell after death, as it tended to choose heaven or hell in any moment while alive.

Although a devout Christian, Swedenborg proclaimed (like most illumined souls) the universal validity of all religions, saying they "are like so many jewels in a King's crown." He said the true church existed wherever people acted in charity toward one another, and all would be saved, no matter what their faith, who lived by the principle of love. Without love, he observed, we are nothing.

Swedenborg swore that the angels in heaven revealed these truths to him. His mystical writings achieved fame and notoriety in his lifetime. Yet he published and sold them anonymously, at less than printing costs, and at his own expense. His sole purpose was to spread spiritual truth to as many people as possible, as he had been assigned by heaven. His authorship was, in fact, only discovered near the end of his life. His voluminous works, translated into twenty languages and still in print after two centuries, have influenced numerous writers, artists, and mystics, among them Balzac, Hugo, Blake, Emerson, Thoreau, Whitman, Jung, D. T. Suzuki, Alan Watts, and many more. A worldwide church of Swedenborgian Christianity exists today.

Many inspired leaders have had premonitions of their deaths. But Swedenborg predicted the year, day, and hour of his death to his intimate circle. When Swedenborg was on his deathbed, a clergyman named Fernelious came to administer last rites. He told Swedenborg that many people believed he had created his spiritual writings from his own imagination, and that if this were the case he ought to confess it before he died and depart with a clean conscience. Wrote Fernelious:

Swedenborg thereupon half rose in his bed, and laying his hand upon his breast said with some manifestation of zeal: "As true as you see me before your eyes, so true is everything that I have written; and I could have said more had it been permitted. When you enter eternity, you will see everything, and then you and I shall have much to talk about."

After his death, the maid of the house in which Swedenborg lived said he had seemed to be looking forward to the event with great enthusiasm, "as if he were going on holiday." After a lifetime of extraordinary service, and knowing full well his destination, perhaps he was.

SKINHEAD TO GODHEAD

Redemption of a Racist

When he was thirteen, Richard Sabinski attended church three times. After each visit, he would talk about God with his friends. But Richard was a troubled and angry youth. Although he spoke of God with fervor, he hated all people of other races. At fifteen, his churchgoing days long past, Richard started doing drugs and getting into fights and other trouble. Pushing drugs by sixteen, he soon had three friends selling for him. Later he bought a gun and pistol-whipped a man named Terry who refused to pay for some drugs. He then fired several shots into the side of Terry's car.

Terry escaped and called the police, who arrested Richard, only to release him when Terry declined to press charges. A few days later, Richard saw Terry riding in a truck and began tailgating him. A high-speed chase ensued in which Richard fired his gun out his window at the fleeing car. Richard was arrested again and this time was sentenced to eight years in prison.

The overcrowded prison, brimming with racial tension, was a war zone where hatreds were color-coded and violence a part of everyday life. Blacks, whites, and Hispanics fought territorial wars and formed gangs for protection. Skin colors became the uniforms of opposing armies, and racism became a bond of brotherhood. Richard's hatred of nonwhites now deepened to a burning focus, and his gang became a potent symbol of his identity. In prison Richard received a criminal education that he would draw upon after his release less than two years later due to overcrowded prison conditions.

Back on the streets at nineteen, Richard returned to the drug business, now with hard-core members of his prison alma mater as his fellow travelers on a dark path — armed robbers, drug users, violent felons. Richard even attended one satanic ritual involving drugs, wild dancing, and formal prayers to Satan.

As Richard described it:

> *By the time I was twenty-three years old, I realized I was an evil person. This reflection struck me out of nowhere — I was in my backyard, suddenly overcome by great sadness about my life and what I'd become. I knelt down and asked God for mercy. It was the first time I'd prayed in ten years. The next day I told several friends I was going to start over and become a new person. They laughed their teeth out.*

Three days later, after finishing some Chinese food at a friend's house, Richard opened his fortune cookie to find the message "Do not leave the righteous path you have chosen."

But Richard wasn't yet ready to hear this prophetic message. That same night he and his friends went bowling and spied six Asian men a few lanes away. Richard's reflexive hatred welled up inside him — any skin color besides white made him see red. He and his friends approached the Asians and started a fight. But two black men stepped in to defend them. Outnumbered, Richard and his friends left, raging about "niggers" and "gooks."

A few days later Richard stood again in his backyard:

It was just getting dark when I heard the sound of a bugle somewhere above me. I looked up and saw the sky split right in half. It was the eeriest thing I'd ever seen; one side of the sky was light and the other side dark. I knew without a doubt that God was asking me to change — giving me a choice. Again I saw the darkness inside me, but this time I also saw a shaft of light, a ray of hope. I knelt down and again asked God to forgive me. All the violence, the hatred and craziness of my life flashed through my mind — all of it. I saw what a miracle it was that I had survived. I felt so grateful to be alive. I suddenly understood what a gift life is. And I knew that I wanted to do something good with mine.

Richard's vision changed his character overnight:

The next day, I went to the bus stop and saw a black man waiting there alone. I looked at him and was amazed — I felt no hatred toward him. I saw he was a human being just like me. I'd never looked at a nonwhite person without that rage rising in me. Now the rage was gone. I was so surprised. I almost started to cry. He turned toward me. I smiled and said, "Hello." It was the first kind word I had ever spoken to a black man. Overnight my heart had turned from stone to flesh. From that moment on, I haven't felt any racial hatred for another person.

Soon after that, Richard quit drugs, stopped fighting, and began to experience a new way of life — a brotherhood with all people. Still, he met with practical life challenges, with tests and trials. "I had to find a new way to make a living, to stabilize my life. I was poor for a while," he said.

During this period of soul-searching, Richard happened to see a Chinese man on television with fingers missing on each of his hands. The man had been tortured and persecuted for his religious activities. Deeply moved by this man's story, Richard realized that, for reasons beyond his understanding, he had been given a special compassion for the Chinese people. He resolved, then and there, to go to China to help them.

Following the call of his heart, Richard Sabinski learned to speak Mandarin and went to wander through China, teaching English and reaching out a helping hand in friendship to strangers of another race he had formerly despised.

WHEN THE SUN DANCED

New Light on the Miracle at Fatima

In 1915, Lúcia Santos, an eight-year-old shepherd girl in Fatima, Portugal, was reciting the rosary near her flock when a human form shimmering within a luminous cloud appeared to her. According to her testimony, the apparition visited her three more times that year.

If it had ended there, such visitations might have been dismissed as the active stirrings of a young girl's imagination. But the following year the same shining form appeared to Lúcia and to her two young cousins, Francisco and Jacinta Marto. The children had sought shelter from a storm in a small cave. While playing near the cave entrance, they heard a distant roar and looked out over the trees in the valley below to see a sphere of white light, like a glowing cloud, soaring toward them. When it stopped to hover nearby, they saw an angel within — an exquisitely beautiful young man.

"I am the Angel of Peace," he said. He taught them a prayer, then vanished. In a rapture, the children repeated the prayer for hours until they swooned with exhaustion.

The angel returned that summer and urgently told the children to pray. The following autumn, he again appeared in the cave and administered Communion before departing. Each time, over-whelmed by this mysterious apparition, the children fell into a deep, trancelike state.

For a while the children kept these visits a secret. But in 1917, the "three children's miracle" became a series of mass events — supernatural encounters with an awesome power that transformed the lives of nearly one hundred thousand people, and indirectly, millions more. The following chronicle highlights these recurring visitations, each viewed by growing crowds of awestruck wit-nesses.

On May 13, the three shepherd children were surprised by a flash of brilliant white light. They walked toward it into a nearby hollow pasture and were momentarily blinded by a bright, glow-ing sphere, in the midst of which stood a tiny woman. She told them she came from heaven, and asked them to return to the same spot each month thereafter.

A month later to the day, the children returned as requested. This time fifty people accompanied them. The witnesses saw the children kneel and speak to thin air, their faces transfigured with unearthly light. The children all saw the lady of light as Mary, Mother of Christ. The meeting ended with a loud explosion. Then a small cloud of light, visible to all, rose above the tree beside which the children knelt.

The following month a crowd of forty-five hundred people watched the children converse with the air. Many heard a buzzing drone; the sun grew dim and lost heat, and then a small luminous cloud materialized around the tree and, with a sharp explosion, departed toward the east.

The children revealed several prophecies made by the lady in the cloud, all of which came true. She told them that the present war would soon end — World War I ended a year later — but added, "If people do not stop offending God, another, worse war will begin during the reign of Pius XI" (World War II began in 1939, the last year of Pope Pius's reign). The lady also told the children, "If Russia is not converted, she will spread her errors throughout the world." All these prophecies are documented in records made that same year.

On August 13, 1917, an estimated eighteen thousand people now gathered at the mysterious hollow. The three children were absent, confined by a skeptical official who pressured them to recant their story of Mary's miraculous appearances, or else tell him the secrets she had revealed. When they refused, he separated them and told each that the others had been killed for refusing to talk. Still they remained silent. Meanwhile, the crowd at the hollow heard a loud thunderclap; then, with a bright flash, a luminous cloud formed, rose, and evaporated like mist. High above, the clouds turned the color of blood, then pink, yellow, and blue. The sun shone through, bathing the crowd in mists of rainbow light. Strange petals fell from the sky, vanishing before they touched the ground. The children were released.

Two days later, Lúcia and her cousins were tending their sheep when the temperature dropped abruptly. Once again rainbow colors, witnessed by thousands, filled the countryside. The crowds who now followed the children saw a bright flash, and a luminous cloud enfolded the tree. In the center stood a radiant woman dressed in gold and white. People fell to their knees, "their souls in rapture." The woman spoke to the children and asked them to "make sacrifices for sinners." She then rose into the air and flew slowly east. Those present reported hearing a roaring like the sound of great winds.

On September 13, a small army of thirty thousand now-converted souls blanketed the meadows around the tree in the hollow where the children waited. Around noon the sun dimmed, though the sky was clear. The air erupted with the cries of thousands as a luminous sphere approached from the east and descended to rest upon the tree by the children. The sphere became a cloud from which shining petals fell once again, melting away to nothing before touching the outstretched hands of the multitude. The lady in the center of the sphere spoke with Lúcia, promising a miracle on the thirteenth day of October. She then ascended in her cocoon of light, and before the eyes of the astonished onlookers, sped straight up and disappeared into the sun. Among the thousands of witnesses were two priests who had come specifically to expose the now-famous miracles as a sham. The two devout skeptics were converted on the spot.

By October 13, the day of the prophesied miracle, word had spread far and wide. Seventy thousand people stood in the pouring rain beneath thick gray clouds surrounding the hollow where the children sat. At noon came a flash of light accompanied by "a strange sweet fragrance." The three children, their faces radiant, conversed briefly with the lady in the sphere of light.

Then the apparition ascended, the rain stopped, and the thick clouds parted dramatically. The sun now appeared as a shining silver disk. As thousands of witnesses later testified, the silver sun spun rapidly, throwing off brilliant beams of colored light in all directions. Fatima author William Thomas Walsh interviewed many witnesses, and recounted the event as it was described to him:

> *While they gazed, the huge ball began to "dance."... Now it whirled rapidly like a gigantic fire-wheel for some time with dizzy, sickening speed. Finally there appeared on the rim a*

border of crimson, which flung across the sky blood-red stream-
ers of flame, reflecting to the earth, to the trees and shrubs, to
the upturned faces and the clothes all sorts of brilliant colors
in succession: green, red, orange, blue, violet, the whole spec-
trum. Madly gyrating in this manner three times, the fiery orb
seemed to tremble, to shudder, and then to plunge precipi-
tately, in a mighty zigzag, toward the crowd.

Tens of thousands flung themselves upon the muddy earth, praying for their lives and their souls. At the last moment, the disk reversed its apocalyptic descent and the real sun, hidden behind it, appeared above. At tremendous speed, the silver disk ascended and flew into the sun. Incredibly, these events had lasted a full ten minutes. The astonished multitude, drenched only minutes before, found their rain-sodden clothes completely dried. And hundreds of people had been miraculously cured of various injuries and illnesses — cancers, wounds, and crippling diseases. Many went home weeping, shaken to their core.

Thousands of people's lives were profoundly altered that day, including those who had witnessed the miracle from as far away as thirty miles, from which distance the lights in the sky were clearly visible.

Forty-three years later, in 1960, a lawyer named Mendes, who was present at this "miracle at Fatima," testified to what many others also felt about its impact on their lives: "I still remember it today as vividly as at the moment it happened. I feel myself dominated by that extraordinary event."

Thousands of witnesses interviewed in a formal investigation undertaken by the Catholic Church described a wide range of phenomena. Some claimed to have seen two beings on a ladder descending from the sphere. Others saw the moon and stars appear in the sky, though it was midday. Miles away in other villages, people described objects and buildings reflecting the colors of the rainbow. Churches were filled to overflowing in every town.

Today, millions each year visit Fatima, Portugal, now a holy site where miraculous healings still occur. A third and final prophecy revealed to Lúcia by the Lady of Fatima was sealed in an envelope and sent to the Vatican, with instructions that it be opened by the pope in 1960. The envelope was in fact opened.

This third Fatima prophecy remains a matter of controversy to this day.

FREE AS A BIRD

A Gift of Love from Beyond

As far back as he could remember, Boyd Jacobson loved birds. Even as a young boy, raised in rural Washington by his great aunt, Karn — or Mother Karn, as he came to call her — Boyd had spent many hours observing the birds of the Northwest. He loved listening to their calls and collecting feathers, nests, and eggshells.

Boyd's bird-watching expeditions were limited to the fields and meadows near his own backyard, due to his difficulty in walking long distances. As a result of Perthes disease contracted in infancy, Boyd's malformed right leg bone was shorter than his left. He could never walk barefoot without a painful limp. Even with lifts in his shoe, Boyd couldn't run or play sports without aggravating the pain in his hip. But riding a bike was easy, so he became an avid cyclist.

An artist and a free spirit, Boyd eventually moved to Marin County, California, where he worked as a film director. He often rode his bike up the steep and winding paths of his beloved Mt. Tamalpais, a mountain deemed sacred by Native Americans who once populated its pristine slopes.

Boyd was married, and life blessed him with a daughter, Karie.

The marriage eventually ended amicably, and Boyd's relationship with Karie remained close and loving.

Then, in 1989, around Karie's seventeenth year, Boyd met and fell in love with Allison James. Allison also worked in filmmaking. Within a year they were engaged, and they shared a home near Mt. Tam with Karie and with Mother Karn. Allison found Boyd's offbeat, humorous character immensely appealing, and so did most of his friends. Boyd was a witty, off-the-wall original who made people laugh, and his unconventional outlook and manner conveyed an expanded sense of reality.

Even as an adult, Boyd still had a passion for birds. He saw himself as a man, but dreamt of himself as a bird. His friends related to him as "Bird Man." One friend made Boyd a ceramic bird with Boyd's face on it that sat on a perch in a cage and sang when you flipped a switch. "When Boyd left a message on your answering machine," Allison said, "you heard only a birdcall and knew it was a 'Boyd-call.' His business card even featured a cartoon caricature of himself as a bird."

After their engagement, Boyd and Allison decided to go to Bali to plan their wedding. Boyd wanted very much to walk barefoot on the beach with his love without a painful limp, so he decided it was finally time to have the hip operation he needed to repair the degenerated joint. For this routine operation, he decided upon an old college acquaintance as his surgeon. After reassuring his loved ones that all would be well, Boyd Jacobson went under anesthesia. But he never regained consciousness due to a tragic surgical mishap.

His completely unexpected passing devastated everyone who had loved him, especially Allison, Karie, and Mother Karn. Even more heartbreaking, Boyd had left without saying good-bye.

After he was cremated, half of Boyd's ashes were sent to his family's plot in Washington. Allison and Karie decided to scatter his remaining ashes in his favorite meadow atop his beloved Mt. Tam. Two of Boyd's friends rode his ashes up on the back of his mountain bike along his favorite trail. Allison and Karie drove ahead to the top and chose a beautiful spot in the meadow near two granite boulders. After Boyd's friends arrived, they performed a simple ceremony, then scattered his ashes across the meadow.

Several weeks after Boyd's death, Allison had a vivid dream: She was on foot doing an errand for her movie studio and heard Boyd's unmistakable birdcall nearby. She entered a store and followed his call to the back, where she found him. He spoke to her for a while, and told her to "do the right thing." Before the dream ended, Boyd held out her cat Chelsea's food dish in one hand, saying he knew she was hungry. Then playfully he held out his other fist, which he turned and opened. Sitting on his palm was a small white bird — a dream gift for Allison.

Allison awoke feeling strongly that she'd actually met Boyd's spirit. Chelsea was meowing hungrily, her cat dish empty. For Allison, Boyd's message, "Do the right thing," meant that she should take care of Mother Karn, then eighty-seven, for the rest of her life, as he would have done. Allison made an inner promise to Boyd to do just that. She later shared her dream with Karie and Karn.

Days later, Karie was going through Boyd's things in another room when Allison heard her exclaim, "Oh, my god!" Karie, holding out her closed fist, came up to Allison and said, "This must be for you." Then Karie turned her hand over and opened it. In her palm sat a small white ceramic bird. They both had goose bumps, and tears formed in Allison's eyes.

Then, two months after Boyd's death, Allison got a phone call from Glenn, a friend of Boyd's from out of town who had missed the memorial. Glenn was coming to town and wanted to visit Boyd's meadow on Mt. Tam. So Glenn, Karie, Allison, and her friend Barbara drove up together and parked the car at the trailhead.

Glenn and Karie took separate trails for some private time, so Allison and Barbara reached the meadow first and approached the first of two granite boulders marking his site. There on the farthest boulder, six feet away, sat a large and beautiful pure white bird, gazing directly at them. Allison and Barbara froze, so as not to frighten the bird away, then looked at each other in astonishment. They sat down near the boulder nearest to them.

Immediately the bird flew onto their rock, only a few feet from Allison. On impulse, she reached out her hand and made a come-here gesture. With a hop and a flutter, the bird flew into Allison's lap. Instinctively she felt the bird was a message from Boyd, like the white bird in the palm of his hand in her dream, and the white bird that Karie brought to her from his belongings. In that moment, she felt a profound shift in her grieving process; a torn place in her soul had begun to mend. It seemed that somehow Boyd had sent this bird as an emissary of comfort and a way to say farewell — evidence that his spirit was alive and free as a bird.

Allison sat still for forty-five minutes, stroking the bird. Barbara, as well as Karie and Glenn, sat quietly with them. It felt like a spontaneous ceremony, an experience of grace and wonder. Finally, Allison said good-bye and thanked the bird, thanked Boyd, thanked the universe, and prepared to hike back to the car. Allison stood up slowly, expecting the bird to fly off. Instead, the bird hopped up and perched on her shoulder. Amazed, she headed down the trail with her new feathered friend.

After some distance, Allison gently lifted the bird and put it on Karie's shoulder so she too could physically feel this living link to her father. Karie took about twenty steps down the trail, then stopped and looked back. As she did so, the bird flew back onto Allison's shoulder, where it stayed.

The afternoon grew chilly as the four of them approached the car, with plans to drive down the mountain into Mill Valley for a warming cup of coffee in a local café. Allison once again told the bird good-bye — clearly she couldn't take it with her. But this bird was going nowhere. It remained steadfast on Allison's shoulder as she got into the car, drove down the mountain, walked into the café, sat down at a table, and had a cappuccino. The bird was still on Allison's shoulder when she and Karie walked into the house to tell the story and introduce Boyd's emissary to Mother Karn.

More than seven years later, in 1998, Allison, Karn, and Karie were living in their own separate homes. The white bird, now called Birdie, was still living with Allison, a part of the family. Allison built a comfortable indoor cage for Birdie, but from the beginning let her feathered friend know it was free to fly as it wished. She often let the bird out for the run of the house, and Birdie often followed Allison outside when she worked in the garden. Birdie never flew out of Allison's sight.

After some research, Allison decided that Birdie was a great American king dove, but she couldn't tell if Birdie was male or female. Then, during the week of the first anniversary of Boyd's death, Birdie laid a single white egg — small enough to hold in the palm of your hand, or hide in a closed fist.

Birdie, a gift from Boyd, revealed to Allison more clearly than ever that the universe is a mysterious place, and that death is not the end of life or of love.

CONVERSION BY LIGHTNING

A Prisoner's Sudden Realization

Huang Yao Rong was born in Sichuan Province in 1930s' China. His family, too poor to raise him, sent him to Hong Kong to live with his aunt, the wife of an officer in the Kuomintang party, then fighting the Chinese Communists for control of China. In Hong Kong, Huang received a British education, and after graduating from college, returned to China to work for the Canton Railway.

In the early 1950s, the Communists won the revolution, defeating the Kuomintang, whose members fled to Taiwan. Huang's political status was now tainted by his Kuomintang uncle and aunt. To make matters worse, he had been baptized a Christian in 1946. Like millions of other politically suspect Chinese citizens, Huang lived under the party's close supervision.

With his engineering skills needed for China's modernization, Huang was allowed to work in relative freedom. But as stormy political movements swept through China, Huang was often publicly criticized and twice arrested for alleged criminal political activities. Then, on August 10, 1968, in the frenzied violence of China's Cultural Revolution, Huang was arrested as a spy. With his hands and feet bound and a dunce cap on his head, he was beaten and dragged through the streets before jeering crowds, then put in a makeshift military prison in his workplace. His fellow employees became his prison guards.

Millions across China suffered similar fates. Hundreds of thousands of warehouses, auditoriums, and buildings were converted into makeshift prisons after the established prisons were filled. Each morning and afternoon at public meetings, Huang was forced to kneel for hours at a time, head bowed, while he was verbally and physically abused. Each night he was forced to write "self-criticism reports" confessing to political crimes he had never committed. Refusal to confess was considered proof of guilt, and punished by beatings.

When Huang grew uncooperative, his hands, feet, three ribs, and an arm were broken, his lower vertebrae were fractured, and his skull was cracked. The skin on much of his body, raw and bloody from his beatings, stung with sweat in the summer's heat. Unrelenting nightly interrogations blended terror and pain as muscular youths pounded his chest and ribs, continuing even when he began vomiting blood. Unable to walk, Huang had to be dragged to and from his cell. Denied medical attention, he was forced to sit upright in his cell around the clock and allowed a single, one-minute bathroom break per day. He lost control of his bladder and bowels and soiled himself daily.

So passed his first fifteen days of captivity.

Then, one grim night in August 1968, a monsoon hit Canton. Thunder and lightning shook Huang's cell, and the fierce gusts shattered his window. Huang described what happened next:

I was sitting against the wall. In the dim light I looked down and saw myself covered with blood and filth. After all the

*beatings I no longer had the shape of a human being. I knew
if it continued I would die. So I decided not to wait for death,
but finish it myself, out of hatred for my enemies and to end
my pain. Once this idea rose in me, I began to think of my
wife and mother. My heart was in chaos. My emotions rose to
a desperate pitch. Clenching my teeth I took a shard of glass
from the window broken by the crazy monsoon winds. My
hands shook uncontrollably as I began to cut the artery in my
left wrist.*

*The next moment, thunder exploded nearby and a bolt of
lightning flashed in my cell through the broken window. In
that same instant, a bright light lit up my heart — this is the
only way to describe it. I woke up. I saw clearly that my life
was sacred, given to me by a divine power — I had no right
to destroy myself.*

*Many things were revealed to me in that instant. I saw the
divisions and hatreds that had torn my country apart. My
guards and torturers believed I was evil, as I believed they
were. Our mutual hatred seemed justified. Now I saw that as
long as I hated them, the cycle would continue. Not even my
death would end it. Only love could end hatred. And I could
choose love. In that life-and-death moment I realized no human effort, only a greater power, could save me and resolve my
situation. I had not prayed in twenty years. Now I knew the
only way out of this alley of death was through repentance and
prayer.*

Abruptly, Huang's rage toward his torturers had vanished. He
now saw clearly that these fanatical idealists, mostly in their teens
and early twenties, had been raised in "revolutionary cradles" and
taught to hate their enemies. Despite the terrible pain and cruelty

they had inflicted upon him, Huang's heart overflowed with compassion. He now understood Christ's words on the cross: "Father, forgive them, for they know not what they do."

Huang prayed through the night as thunder roared, lightning flashed, and rain washed in through the broken window. When the day broke, the storm outside, and the storm within Huang Yao Rong's heart, had subsided. The suicidal despair and emotional agony of the last fifteen days had been lifted from him, replaced by a newfound serenity, clarity, and faith. Huang consciously sensed a divine power working on him from within.

Blessed with courage, Huang requested paper and pen and with his broken hand scrawled a letter to the head of the military control committee, describing without rancor his present condition and the torture he had endured. He felt no animosity toward his tormentors now — only their shared humanity. Soon the young guards began to treat him differently. They gave him a chair during his interrogations. They beat him a few more times after that, but not harshly. The torture ceased altogether. He was fed better and was allowed to go to the bathroom whenever he needed, to shower, and to write to his family.

Huang spent five more years in prison before being pronounced innocent and released. Five years later he was officially exonerated. Due to spinal and head injuries sustained during his torture, he eventually lost the use of the right side of his body.

In 1997, Huang, now living in the United States, visited Canton. There, one of his old friends and fellow workers told him the following story: Several months earlier, a worker dying of brain cancer — a former guard in their workplace prison — had confessed to him that during the Cultural Revolution he had severely tortured and maimed two individuals. One of them was Huang Yao

Rong. "I have had no peace ever since," the dying man said. "I had to tell someone." He passed away several days later.

The friend asked Huang, crippled from his torture thirty years before, if he hated the people who had done this to him. "No," Huang replied. "If I hate, I lose my peace; if I forgive, I am given peace. How futile my hatred would have been toward a man who all these years suffered such remorse over his actions."

Huang Yao Rong remarked:

Everything happened just as I have said. I have witnessed and experienced divine blessings beyond what I have the power to describe. Despite my severe physical handicap, I have found great happiness and peace. I have hope. I rely on the supreme wisdom of the divine to lead me through every difficult passage. I pray every day. I live to do God's work. I have sometimes made mistakes. But I have never forsaken my faith.

MIND OVER MATTER

From Sickly Child to Superhuman

O n the sweltering evening of July 15, 1893, in the poorest section of Suvalk, Poland, Chaya Greenstein fell while carrying water home. She went into labor and soon gave birth to a three-and-a-half-pound boy, three months premature. In those times, premature infants rarely survived, especially among the poor. So when this tiny child survived his first week, nursed with an eye dropper, sleeping in a cotton-lined bed the size of a shoe box, word spread. Three doctors who visited the child concluded that there was nothing they could do. Yet the baby, struggling for breath, too weak to cry out, clung to life. Finally he was given a name: Yoselle, or Joseph.

Six years passed. Young Joseph, now a frail boy cared for by his mother — his father had died the year before — walked to school through the winter snow, his feet wrapped in rags. Pale and congested — an asthmatic like his late father — Joseph struggled to endure in the face of his physical infirmities. But in his fourteenth winter, after a medical examination, Joseph overheard the doctor tell his mother that he wasn't likely to reach his eighteenth birthday. He watched his mother fighting to hold back her tears.

On the way home from the doctor's office, while passing a small array of circus tents, Joseph noticed a poster featuring a strongman with muscles like marble. Beneath the poster were the words *Champion Volanko*. Enthralled by the picture — an image of health, strength, and vitality — Joseph begged his mother to let him visit the show. Sadly, she had no money for admission.

Joseph somehow knew that he *had* to see this champion. So when he spied some boys sneaking in under the tent, he did the same — and found himself face-to-face with a circus roustabout who began to beat and kick him. In the next moment, out of nowhere, Champion Volanko himself appeared, stopped the beating, and befriended young Joseph. The few words Volanko spoke struck the sickly youth with a force that would change the course of his life: "I was once more sickly than you," Volanko said. "The greatest athletes have often grown from the weak and infirm." Then he asked Joseph directly, "Do you want to die?"

Joseph wanted very much to live, and he asked Volanko to show him how. So the strongman became a mentor to the weakling, a father to a fatherless boy.

That night Joseph bid his mother a tearful good-bye. Filled with hope — for he had little else — Joseph left town with the circus as Volanko's helper and disciple. Sometimes life-changing moments come in the form of an angel of light, and sometimes in the form of a Jewish circus strongman with a thick Russian accent and muscles like carved marble.

Joseph learned two important things from Volanko that he would never forget: First, he must assume no limitations; second, he must stretch each day beyond what he believed he could do. When the muscular strongman stood in the snow lifting heavy weights, naked except for a loincloth, the skinny boy watched, enthralled by Volanko's vitality. Emulating Volanko, Joseph rubbed snow on his bare flesh and lifted empty buckets, which, over time, Volanko gradually filled with sand — a handful more each day. From his teacher, Joseph learned to eat nourishing grains, to train hard, and to kill his illness before it had a chance to kill him. Volanko taught Joseph practical knowledge as well as spiritual wisdom: "It is hard to be a Jew, hard to be a man, but you must do your best."

Joseph learned about his mind and spirit as he learned to wrestle. His racking cough began to fade with his old life as he practiced deep breathing. He kept pushing beyond, challenging the limits of his mind and body.

"Always think just one more, just one more," Volanko urged.

In Ed Spielman's classic "biography of a superhuman," *The Spiritual Journey of Joseph L. Greenstein: The Mighty Atom*, he reveals how Joseph traveled across Europe and the East to learn mental disciplines and training methods that enabled him to perform extraordinary feats of strength seldom accomplished before and rarely duplicated since.

These feats included biting steel nails in half; bursting heavy chains by expanding his chest; bending heavy iron rods with his fingers; making finger rings out of twenty-penny nails; twisting two-inch steel bars around his arm; playing with three-hundred-pound dumbbells as if they were children's toys; supporting a large horse, cow, and four men on his chest while lying on a bed of nails; pulling a twenty-ton fire truck with twenty men on it around the block; driving twenty-penny nails through a two-inch plank with one blow of his bare fist; bending iron bars over the bridge of his nose while supporting four people; straightening horseshoes with his bare hands, then breaking them in two; swinging a "merry-go-round" of six people all hanging from his long hair; and preventing two powerful automobiles from driving off in opposite directions by holding them back with a rope in each hand.

Yet even these amazing feats of power were not Joseph's most impressive demonstrations of mind over matter. After much preparation in strengthening his scalp, Joseph fastened his hair to a rope and the rope to a chain, which he attached to a new Fairchild FC-2 airplane powered by a nine-cylinder engine identical to the one Charles Lindbergh had flown in to cross the Atlantic sixteen months before. Then Joseph accomplished something the experts had said was not humanly possible: He stood on the runway behind the plane, which revved its engine to over 1600 rpm trying to take off. Joseph stood his ground and held the machine in place. (Later, a powerful young stuntman died attempting the same feat.)

Joseph Greenstein's photos reveal a physically fit man of small stature — a few inches over five feet. His physique looks quite modest when compared to the hulking, high-tech muscles of today's bodybuilders and power lifters. Yet none of today's strongmen can begin to approach Joseph's apparently superhuman feats. His abilities emanated more from his faith and spirit than from his muscles.

And the source of his power also provided incredible support and protection, as demonstrated by the following incident: On October 12, 1914, a disturbed youth, enamored of Joseph's wife, Leah, fired a .38-40 caliber revolver point-blank at Joseph. The bullet struck Joseph between the eyebrows, knocking him off his feet. He lay stunned, blood running down his face, knowing he had been shot between the eyes. Finally he put his thumb against the bullet hole to stem the flow of blood, rose to his feet, and staggered across the street to the pharmacy. As he went in, several patrons ran out; one fainted. The druggist, who had seen gunshot wounds before, took one look and said, "You alive?"

"I'm talking to you, aren't I?" Joseph replied.

Later in the emergency room the doctor found the bullet flattened against Joseph's skull; it had barely penetrated the bone.

"I was shot between the eyes," said Joseph. "Why am I alive?"

The doctors had no explanation. The incident was investigated and reported by three Houston newspapers on Tuesday, October 13, 1914 — by the *Press*, the *Chronicle*, and the *Daily Post*. The facts, as reported, were straightforward: A real bullet from a working pistol had been fired at close range into Joseph Greenstein's forehead. The result: a small indentation in his skull, and scarcely more than a flesh wound.

Following this apparent miracle, Joseph began to question his larger purpose in life. He shared the fruits of his contemplation with his wife: "Leah, I was on the ground; I knew I was shot; then somehow I wasn't myself, but something much more. I knew in that instant that I would not die, that I could not die — not yet. It is for a reason, Leah. Everything . . . Volanko, the bullet, everything."

After this extraordinary experience, second only to his meeting with Champion Volanko, Joseph began his incarnation as the Mighty Atom, who would go on to inspire people all over the world by demonstrating not merely the power of his body, but the power of the human mind and spirit.

Once a premature infant fed with an eye dropper, Joseph became not only the strongest man on earth but also a loving and faithful husband; a father to ten children; a showman, citizen, and inventor; and a lecturer on physical culture and health — a man of his time and beyond his time.

By harnessing a force from beyond the physical realm, Joseph Greenstein, the Mighty Atom, showed a way to transcend apparent limits by uniting the powers of mind, will, courage, and spirit. Until Joseph passed away, he continued to inspire and teach all who came to him. He would have made Champion Volanko, the generous strongman who intervened in Joseph's life, very proud indeed.

A SOLDIER'S HEALING

Vietnam Vet to Inspired Dramatist

S ean Kilcoyne was born in the industrial city of Worcester, Massachusetts, in 1946 to a blue-collar, Irish Catholic factory-working family. He attended church faithfully and served Mass as an altar boy for four years. Sean planned to be a priest, but changed his mind at the age of twelve after viewing the prospect of lifelong celibacy from the vantage point of puberty. Instead, he transferred his religious fervor into the secular arena and became the youngest Eagle Scout in the history of Massachusetts.

As a teenager, Sean did summer work in factories, making nails and disemboweling chickens. He struggled through three high schools, finally graduated with honors, and was accepted into Holy Cross College. Feeling isolated in the elite, upper-middle-class atmosphere, despite his election as school vice president, Sean quit after the first year and returned to factory work. Then in 1966 he was drafted.

Like most Americans of that era, Sean had barely heard of Vietnam. By now a lapsed Catholic with an innate opposition to war, he filed three appeals at his draft board to avoid military service. When the appeals were refused, he joined the Marines, thinking the

Marines' discipline would improve his chances of survival. When Sean was ordered to Vietnam, he made a private vow that if he survived, he would create some meaningful art out of his war experience.

Sean arrived in Da Nang near Monkey Mountain as part of an ammunition convoy. That first day his battalion drove into the countryside, past long lines of peasants on the side of the road carrying baskets and produce on their heads and bicycles. These wary peasants watched the soldiers with fear and resentment in their eyes. An eerie, unnerving scene followed: Sean saw soldiers swinging their rifles like golf clubs from the trucks. One broke a woman's arm; she wailed and clutched her maimed limb. Another soldier laughed and slammed his rifle butt into the back of an old man's head, knocking him down.

Repulsed by this inhumanity, Sean wept, feeling a shock of grief and fear that would haunt him far beyond the one year, one month, and one day of his remaining tour of duty in Vietnam. "The people I thought we'd come to help saw us as a malignant force — a significant part of their suffering — and they were right."

The constant fear, the war's carnage, and a growing collective sense of futility, disillusion, and betrayal took their toll on the young soldiers in this land far from home. They had entered a war where success was measured by body counts, where their lives were routinely gambled in reckless bids to increase already-inflated statistics, where the enemy was a guerrilla army that attacked by surprise, then hid in the jungles.

The Vietnam War became notorious for creating a culture of self-medicating drug abuse. Sean and his friends got drunk and stoned every night, and a substance-induced facade of sanity was maintained.

After Sean's service culminated during the Tet Offensive, he returned home with a serious drug and alcohol habit. He walked his old neighborhood streets listening for the sound of gunfire that never came. His life had taken on a disorienting, surreal quality. One day, walking down a clean suburban street, he felt all the houses were upside-down. Alcohol seemed to help him manage his unnerving perceptions.

With dreams of changing the system, Sean returned to college on the G.I. Bill and graduated with a political science degree. As Director of Research for Urban Affairs in the Massachusetts legislature, he led a team that coauthored a bill providing subsidized housing for the elderly. Sean seemed a natural for politics — until one day a reporter asked Sean if he planned to run for office. He replied, "I'm hesitant, but flexible." The next day he read his own words in the newspaper and was disgusted by their "cunning ambiguity." Sean dropped out; he moved to France to write, make art, and pursue his drinking.

Within a year he was living on the streets of Paris, warming his hands in the morning fires of ash cans. The war continued to fill his thoughts and haunt his dreams. The war Sean had left behind still raged inside him. So he moved to Guatemala and tried to lose himself in Mayan indigenous villages. But one day he woke up lying drunk on the ground in a jungle village, and realized he was still trying to get back to Vietnam. It would take him years to understand why.

In 1976 Sean flew to Haight Ashbury, San Francisco. The Summer of Love was long past, and the Haight was now a paranoid pharmaceutical asylum. Sean recalled:

I drank and did drugs and hung out in strange bars with guys who locked themselves in their rooms, ate only cabbage, and

worried about the FBI slipping microphones under their doors.
Every day I woke up, got drunk and high. By late morning
I'd be on the floor, howling under a mattress I'd pulled on top
of myself. During the day I walked the streets jabbering,
angry, talking to myself about the lies, betrayal, and slaugh-
ter of the war. I was still in the jungle, on my way to becom-
ing a village idiot. At night I sat in front of my space heater,
contemplating suicide. But refusing to die was the only thing
that gave me a sense of power.

Then, one spring afternoon in 1978, as Sean walked aimlessly
through the streets of San Francisco in a state of despair, he
stopped at the curb for a red light on the corner of Ninth and Mar
ket Streets.

Both the light, and his life, were about to change.

Sean described what happened next:

I looked up and saw a young angel, six inches tall, in white
trousers, hovering in the air a foot off from my right temple. He
was bare-chested, had white wings growing out of his back,
and held a sledgehammer in his hands, which he pounded
silently on an anvil. Then I saw an identical angel off my left
temple, also silently pounding a hammer on an anvil. In a
flash, I felt a shock of awe as I saw my own darkness, and
fully opened to the wound at my center. I experienced the depth
of desperation and savage anxiety that had driven me for
years.

In that moment, I knew I wasn't alone — that my life
wasn't going to end this way. As I gazed at these angels,
incredible serenity filled me. These beings were aware of me,
had come to help me, to protect me. I felt a quality of love and
attention I'd never experienced before. These angels, pounding

on their anvils, sent energy surging through my body. Some-
how this vision told me I had toughness and mettle. They
saved my life.

The angels' intervention opened a calm space around Sean. He drank less as he pondered his vision and his life, examining his self-destructive patterns, considering how else he might live. He sought help at a veterans' hospital and began to confront his war trauma. Soon Sean quit drinking and drugs, and joined a therapy group with twenty vets. This was 1979, when the new syndrome of post-traumatic stress disorder (PTSD) was just being identified.

"Vietnam was the source of a sacred wound for many of us," Sean said in retrospect. "For years it was my only connection with reality. I needed to somehow touch its significance, to keep it alive until I could deal with it."

Sean and others in his group joined a community-based veterans' organization called Swords to Plowshares. They began to devise tools for dealing with PTSD and worked with other traumatized vets — soldiers with "the thousand-yard stare," which came to be called "frozen mourning." Sean later created a mental health unit that contributed to our nation's understanding of PTSD.

As his healing continued, Sean recalled his former vow to make meaningful art out of his war experience; he also resolved to create a meaningful life out of his angelic vision. Fascinated with the mysteries of language, symbols, dreams, and sacred images — wanting to understand "the knowledge behind the knowledge," the hidden truths that give life meaning — Sean began creating ritual or sacred theater. First performing in the streets with other likeminded artists, he eventually began working with a professional group whose critically acclaimed pieces toured major U.S. and European cities. He also cocreated a performance piece called

Angels/Anvils, dedicated to his life-changing vision. On tour in 1989, *Angels/Anvils* received both popular and critical acclaim.

In 1990, Sean pursued his vision of "the theater of healing" by organizing a reconciliation ritual at the San Francisco War Memorial, with both American and North Vietnamese war veterans, some of whom came from Vietnam to participate in the event. In 1991, during the Gulf War, Sean conceived and directed *The Boon*, a "performance grieving ritual" for war veterans and people of the Middle East, with Robert Bly, Malidoma Patrice Somé, Matthew Fox, and others.

Sean Kilcoyne went on to work as an avant-garde artist and "a grateful agent of conscious evolution." Of his life and work, he said, "On my way to die, I was brought back and given a life. I keep faith with my vision by healing and creating. This is the source of the meaning in my life, and the inspiration for my work."

A LIVING SACRIFICE

The Healings of a Holy Heart

Therese Neumann (1898–1962) exhibited nearly every miraculous phenomena of sainthood in her remarkable and thoroughly documented life. As a Catholic farm girl from a small Bavarian village near the Czechoslovakian border, she led a typical life of chores, school, and church. The eldest of ten children, she cared for a brood of younger siblings. At the age of twelve, she began to hire herself out as a farmer and a domestic to supplement her large family's meager income.

Therese's childhood dream of going to Africa as a missionary ended when she was twenty. First she injured her back, and soon after she tumbled down a flight of stairs. She suffered serious internal injuries, head trauma, and chronic convulsions so severe that they sometimes threw her from her bed. Months after her fall, her deteriorating eyesight failed completely.

She spent the next five years in bed — blind and crippled.

Therese spent these years of darkness and suffering in devotion to Christ, surrendering herself to God's will, and praying with great fervor to her beloved Thérèse of Lisieux, whose saintly life was associated with numerous miracles.

On April 19, 1923, the same day as Thérèse of Lisieux's beatification (formal declaration of blessedness), Therese Neumann, now twenty-five, was lying in her bed in perpetual darkness when she felt a hand touch her. In that instant, her eyesight was fully restored. Soon after this, rose petals from Thérèse of Lisieux's grave, gathered by Neumann's father, were placed in the bandage around Therese's foot. Within several days, the skin, which had rotted away, was restored perfectly.

On May 17, 1925, the day of Thérèse of Lisieux's canonization (formal elevation to sainthood), Therese wrote: "I became aware of a great brightness before my eye. Indescribably beautiful and comforting for the eyes was this light. Then a voice began to speak: 'Wouldn't you like to be well again?'"

Therese answered, "Everything is agreeable to me, whatever my loving God desires — to become well, to remain sick, to die."

The voice told Therese she would be healed, but that she would receive more suffering that no doctor would be able to cure, and that she could help to save other souls.

"Everything the good Lord wants is fine with me," Therese responded.

Therese was instantaneously healed of her paralysis, her crippled legs, and her dislocated vertebrae. Although weakened from seven years of lying in bed, she now rose and walked using a cane.

On September 30 of that same year, the anniversary of Thérèse of Lisieux's death, the radiant light appeared to Therese once again. The voice reminded her of sufferings to come, which she, like Jesus, must bear for the sake of others. "Always remain childlike and simple," the voice admonished.

After that Therese was able to walk without her cane.

On November 13, 1925, Dr. Otto Seidl diagnosed Therese,

now twenty-seven, with acute appendicitis and ordered immediate surgery.

Therese told her priest, "You know, if I tell it to the little Saint, she could help without the cutting."

"Do you really think Saint Thérèse works miracles for you?" the skeptical Dr. Seidl asked. In response, Therese's family gathered rose petals from Saint Thérèse's grave and placed them on Therese's body, this time over her appendix. Then she, her family, and her priest prayed to Saint Thérèse for a miracle. To Dr. Seidl's astonishment, Therese was completely healed within minutes.

Dr. Seidl later testified, "There was no natural explanation for these extraordinary cures and the phenomena that followed them."

On March 28, 1926, directly after Therese had a vision of the Passion of Christ, wounds of the stigmata appeared on her body. At times these stigmata glowed, as documented in photographs. They would remain with her for the rest of her life, and inspire many souls. Hard, nail-shaped protuberances also formed, running through her wounds, creating the uncanny appearance of actual nails driven through her hands and feet. Other wounds appeared: lacerations on her back; those of a crown of thorns around her scalp; and even a deep wound in her side that became an open fissure, like the wound inflicted on the body of Christ by the Roman soldier's spear.

Over the years, many thousands came to see Therese, and many miraculous healings were documented. Therese made clear that she did not heal by her own efforts, but rather by the divine presence and power that emanated from her. She was a vessel of spirit; yet on numerous occasions Therese reportedly appeared to, and miraculously healed, people far away, even across continents, who wrote or prayed to her.

Therese was also seen to levitate during her ecstasies, and on many occasions she was witnessed in two different places at once. When she received Communion, the wafer would at times float from the priest's hand through the air and onto her tongue. At other times the wafer dissolved into thin air before she could swallow it. And in her frequent ecstasies, a wafer sometimes appeared on her tongue out of thin air. Many reliable witnesses testified to these remarkable phenomena.

But perhaps the most extraordinary and well documented of all the unusual phenomena associated with Therese was her total abstinence from any and all food and liquids, other than her one Communion wafer daily. Therese Neumann did not eat or drink for the last forty years of her life — all the more remarkable considering the amount of blood she regularly lost, and the continual pain she endured from her stigmatic wounds. She apparently received her bodily nourishment from a higher power by invisible means, demonstrating the truth that we do not live by bread alone.

These are but a few of the miracles reported in the well-documented history of Therese Neumann. No one, including Therese herself, understood exactly how these things were accomplished. But that they were accomplished was well documented, observed by devotees and skeptics, doctors and scientists alike. In the twentieth century, modern science and timeless faith bore witness to the miraculous life of Therese Neumann — a life of extraordinary experiences that may never be explained.

SCIENTIST OF SACRED ENERGY

An Ordeal of Spiritual Evolution

Controversies have raged for decades between the creationist beliefs of religious fundamentalists and the evolutionary theories of scientific materialists. But according to Gopi Krishna — who applied the scientific method to understand mystical phenomena — there exists a direct but hidden link connecting God and evolution. He reached this conclusion following an ordeal that transformed his life after very nearly ending it.

Gopi was born in a village outside Srinigar, India, in 1903. When Gopi was young, his devout father renounced the world, retreating into a meditative silence from which he never emerged, leaving Gopi's mother to raise the family. Her strength and sacrifice deeply impressed Gopi, her eldest son.

After graduating from high school at seventeen, Gopi entered college. There he spent more time reading for pleasure than preparing for his college examinations, which he failed. Sobered and guilt stricken after his mother's years of sacrifice on his behalf, he vowed to remedy the character flaws — a weak will and lack of mental clarity — that had led to his failure. To improve himself, Gopi rose early each morning to practice meditation and yoga before going to school. What began as a preparation for his academic pursuits became a way of life. But as his character and spiritual nature deepened through these practices, his worldly ambitions faded.

Feeling obligated to support his parents, and wishing to avoid the troubling extremes of his father, Gopi devised a compromise: He fulfilled his worldly duties by day, and devoted himself to spiritual practice by night. After his college graduation at twenty-two, Gopi moved to Kashmir to become a civil servant, taking his parents with him. When he was twenty-three, his mother arranged a marriage for him in the traditional manner, to a bride of sixteen.

For the next twelve years Gopi supported his family, playing the roles of husband, father, and civil servant while continuing his spiritual practices. Then one morning, in December 1937, as he was meditating before work, he noticed an odd sensation stirring and rising at the base of his spine. It ceased, then occurred again. The third time, he ignored it and continued meditating. But it would not be ignored:

> *The sensation again extended upwards, growing in intensity. Suddenly, with a roar like that of a waterfall, I felt a stream of liquid light entering my brain.... The illumination grew brighter and brighter, the roaring louder. I experienced a rocking sensation and then felt myself slipping out of my body, entirely enveloped in a halo of light ... the point of consciousness that was myself growing wider, surrounded by waves of light.... I was now All Consciousness ... immersed in a sea of light, simultaneously aware of every point, spread out, as it were, in all directions.*

This experience left Gopi exhausted, nervous, and strangely depressed. The next morning the experience repeated itself with equal intensity. He didn't yet know his life had forever changed, nor that a twelve-year ordeal had begun — one in which he would teeter precariously between life and death, madness and sanity.

Gopi interpreted the event as the awakening of kundalini, the spiritual energy that resides, according to Hindu scripture, at the base of the spine. This event, sought by many in the East as the goal of spiritual practice, triggered a bewildering process in Gopi, who now found himself assaulted from within by a torrent of disturbing and extraordinary phenomena: Day and night his mind became a theater of visions, of visible patterns of light, of force and sounds entering his brain in a continuous stream. He could not concentrate, sleep, or eat. He soon lost weight and grew ill. As he described it:

> *I seemed to have accidentally touched the lever of an unknown mechanism hidden in the extremely intricate yet unexplored nervous structure of the body . . . the luminous appearances became wilder and more fantastic and the noises louder and more uncanny. . . . The dreadful thought began to take hold of my mind that I was irretrievably heading towards a disaster from which I was powerless to save myself.*

Weeks passed into months as Gopi's mind swung erratically between torment and exaltation. His body burned on fire from within. In the worst period he lay down in bed each night wondering if he would still be sane — or even alive — in the morning. A growing terror began to alienate him from other people, even his beloved family.

In a desperate search for help, Gopi found a yogi who told him that in rare cases the kundalini rose through the wrong spinal channel, producing hellish and destructive effects, but the yogi didn't know how to undo these effects. Gopi's life-shattering process seemed headed toward a fatal conclusion.

One night Gopi realized he could hold out no longer; he felt madness approaching and death not far behind. Wasted to a skeleton and sleep deprived, his nerves fried, he lay writhing and moaning in agony on his bed, burning up and drenched in sweat. Then, turning his head, he saw his three-year-old daughter watching him, wide-eyed with terror.

In despair, concerned for his daughter and the family he would leave behind, he recalled the yogi's words, and an idea came to him "as if by divine inspiration" about how he might raise the kundalini through the proper spinal channel and save his life. With his own and his family's future at stake, he made the attempt by mentally visualizing this process:

> There was a sound like a nerve thread snapping and instantaneously a silvery streak passed zigzag through the spinal cord, exactly like the sinuous movement of a white serpent in rapid flight, pouring an effulgent, cascading shower of brilliant vital energy into my brain, filling my head with a blissful luster in place of the flame that had been tormenting me.

Now he noticed a tongue of golden flame moving through his body with healing force:

> I lay awake, dumb with wonder, watching this living radiance moving from place to place through the whole digestive tract, caressing the intestines and the liver, while another stream poured into the kidneys and the heart. . . . I watched with boundless gratitude to the Unseen.

The process had radically shifted; the chaotic, destructive force now flowed through Gopi, bathing his cells with a benevolent energy of the highest order. Made sober and cautious by his prior ordeal, he closely studied these new phenomena, more with the wary, objective fascination of a scientist than the exalted hopes of a mystic. "I was in an extraordinary state: a lustrous medium intensely alive and acutely sentient, shining day and night, permeated my whole system, racing through every part of my body ... sure of its path," he said.

This living, organizing, intelligent force seemed to inhabit Gopi's body/mind, commanding his dietary, sleep, and work habits. In exchange for his full cooperation, it rewarded him with astonishing gifts — not the least of which was a kind of "peace that passeth understanding."

Now when he closed his eyes, waking, sleeping, or dreaming, Gopi saw himself enfolded in a mantle of light, felt himself charged with the exquisite current of an exquisite life force. His dreams had become ecstatic visionary voyages to fantastic realms of indescribable splendor. He began to intuit, then perceive, the universe as an infinitely conscious Being. Formerly mundane scenes of the physical world were now imbued with a silvery luster that filled Gopi's eyes with tearful emotion. Ecstatic awe became his "normal" moment-to-moment state.

Then, one day as he walked across a bridge, a new phenomenon occurred:

> *Near me, in a blaze of brilliant light, I felt what seemed to be a conscious Presence ... encompassing me and overshadowing all the objects around, from which two lines of a beautiful verse in Kashmiri poured out to float before my vision, like luminous writing in the air, disappearing as suddenly as they had come.*

Such visions became frequent occurrences — verses appearing before his open eyes, hovering in the air in luminous script, in various languages.

> *The lines occurred one after the other as if dropped into the three-dimensional field of my consciousness ... in fully formed*

*couplets, like falling snowflakes . . . complete with language,
rhyme, and metre. . . .*

Gopi began writing them down. This poetry appeared first
in Kashmiri, then in English, Urdu, Punjabi, Persian, German,
French, Italian, Sanskrit, and Arabic. He had not the slightest
exposure to four of these languages; he simply wrote them down
as visual symbols. Yet when translated, they proved to be not only
grammatically correct but poetically beautiful, full of profound
spiritual insights, and at times precognitive or prophetic in nature.
By the grace of this kundalini force, Gopi Krishna, who had never
written a line of verse, became an accomplished published poet in
ten languages, most of which he did not speak.

Despite the phenomena triggered by his kundalini awakening,
Gopi didn't reveal his experiences or insights until he had observed
this process for a full twenty years. By then he had developed
remarkable expertise on what he called "the evolutionary energy
in man." Rather than seeing his experience as isolated, Gopi
claimed that the entire human species is divinely programmed to
awaken at a certain evolutionary stage. He conceived of kundalini
as the sacred energy of God in the human being, a key to spiritual
awakening, and claimed that kundalini had inspired the great
prophets and sages of history.

Over the next three decades Gopi Krishna wrote nearly twenty
books on the phenomena and significance of kundalini. He tirelessly urged science to investigate this evolutionary power somehow encoded in the human species, operating according to hidden
laws. Once we come to understand it, he believed, both from a scientific and a mystical perspective, we will hold the key to understanding genius, creativity, and even forms of madness. As he
wrote:

Kundalini is a natural but uncommon biological phenomenon ... that leads to the emergence of a conscious personality ... possessing such astounding attributes as to make the phenomenon appear to be the performance of a supernatural agency rather than the outcome of natural but as yet unknown biological laws.

Gopi Krishna saw this superhuman state as one "towards which mankind is evolving irresistibly." His own life supported this assertion: a poor civil servant catapulted from a common state to that visionary paradise of endless creativity and spiritual rapture in which he spent his final years. If Gopi Krishna is correct, both science and religion may need to revise their assessment of our spiritual and evolutionary origins.

UNEXPECTED JOURNEYS

A Businessman Explores Out-of-Body Realms

I n the spring of 1958," wrote Robert Monroe, "I was living a reasonably normal life with a reasonably normal family."

Robert was a successful businessman, a writer of music for television and radio, and an owner of five radio stations with offices on Madison Avenue. Then, with no preparation or apparent reason, he was catapulted beyond his body into realms usually associated with mystics.

Although he could not explain how or why his uncommon adventure began, Robert knew precisely when. One Sunday afternoon, with his wife and two children in church, Robert lay down on the living room couch to take a nap:

I had just become prone when a beam or ray seemed to come out of the sky to the north at about a 30 degree angle from the horizon. It was like being struck by a warm light. . . . The effect when the beam struck my entire body was to cause it to shake violently — to vibrate. I was utterly powerless to move of my own volition. It was as if I were held in a vise.

This same phenomenon repeated itself nine times over the next six weeks — gentle relaxation becoming a sudden violent trembling. Fearing epilepsy or a brain tumor, Robert went to his doctor, who pronounced him in perfect health. But that very night, after he lay down to sleep, it happened again. This time he decided to observe rather than fight this phenomenon. The vibrations swept up and down his body for five minutes, then slowly stopped. Whenever it happened after that, Robert simply witnessed it as objectively as he could. He observed an image of a "flaming electric ring" passing from his head to his feet, sweeping up and down in "a great roaring surge." Robert reported that he could feel the vibrations in his brain.

One night after the now-familiar phenomena occurred, Robert suddenly found himself floating near the ceiling. Disoriented, he first thought the ceiling was a wall. Then he turned over, looked down, and saw his wife in bed with a man lying beside her. It took him a moment to realize that the man was himself.

Until now Robert had feared he might be out of his mind; now it appeared he was out of his body. Thinking that he must be dying, he "dove back in," opened his eyes, got up, and moved around. He felt fine, although stunned by the undeniable reality that "he" was something other than, or at least not limited to, his body.

The vibrations came six more times before Robert dared to try to leave his body again. At his next attempt he came out effortlessly. So began the astral career of Robert Monroe, a modern pioneer who would explore uncharted, nonphysical realms and spaces for decades to come.

Over the next forty years, Robert Monroe was to become the world's premier out-of-body (OOB) researcher. In his meticulous journals and books, he recorded thousands of OOB explorations, detailing the realms he visited and the discoveries he made in his excursions through time and space. He also described various entities he met, from highly evolved spiritual beings and guides to other astral adventurers, lost souls, lucid dreamers, ordinary sleepers in OOB dream states, and even the spirits of the dead.

On one such journey, Robert was drawn to a young bedridden boy around ten years old. The boy, ill and afraid, was aware of Robert's presence. Robert attempted to comfort him, then left, promising to return.

"Several weeks later," Robert wrote, "I left the physical.... The same boy moved into view. He saw me and moved close to me. He was bewildered, but not afraid."

Robert instinctively knew the boy had died.

"What do I do now?" the boy asked him. "Where do I go?" At a loss, Robert put his arm around the boy's shoulder and told him that some "friends" would soon come and take him where he needed to go.

"The next day," Robert said, "the newspaper carried the story of the death of a ten-year-old boy after a lingering illness. He had died in the afternoon, shortly before I had begun the experiment."

What makes Monroe's work especially compelling is the objective methods and technology he used to investigate and verify these decidedly subjective experiences. In the early years he corroborated events in whatever way he could. Once, while sailing out-of-body down the main street of the town where he lived, he noticed a white car up on the grease rack of a local service station, with both back tires removed. Immediately upon returning to his body, he got in his car and drove to the station. There he found the same white car suspended on the racks, the back tires off just as he had seen.

Another weekend afternoon he "visited" a longtime friend and business associate — a woman who knew of his "wild talent." He found her at home with two young women — one blonde and one brunette. They did not see him. Before leaving, Robert gave her a pinch on her side to see if it would have any effect. "She let out a good loud 'Ow!'" he recalled, "and I backed up . . . somewhat surprised. I really hadn't expected to be able to actually pinch her."

The following Monday at work, without telling the woman of his visit, Robert asked her what she had been doing at that time. She had been with two young women — her niece, a brunette, and her niece's friend, a blonde. Robert asked her for more details, but she added nothing more. "Finally, in impatience," Robert wrote, "I asked her if she remembered the pinch. A look of complete astonishment crossed her face."

"Was that you?" she asked, lifting the edge of her sweater to show him "two brown and blue marks at exactly the spot where I had pinched."

"It hurt!" she told Robert, which surprised him, because he had not guessed he could cause a bruise while in his astral body.

Over years of research and experience, a bigger picture began to emerge of the multidimensional nature of the universe, and the various spiritual beings, including ourselves, who inhabit it.

Robert Monroe's three books — beginning with *Journeys Out of the Body* — described a universe of intersecting realms inhabited by nonphysical beings, essentially spirits, who incarnate, or take on bodies, for purposes of higher education, spiritual growth, or even sheer adventure. The human journey begins, said Monroe, with a soul's disorienting descent into the depths of matter, to the point of total identification with the body and the physical world. Yet the soul is infused with a natural desire to reascend, via spiritual growth, to the blissful freedom of its ultimate home in the light that many call God.

In 1971 Robert Monroe founded the Monroe Institute, a research center devoted to the study of out-of-body phenomena. This was the first time such studies had ever been done using scientific controls and technology — much of which Monroe invented himself.

Over the next two decades, tens of thousands of volunteer researchers, wired and monitored, made hundreds of thousands of journeys, within their minds and often out of their bodies, afterward reporting their findings in great detail. Monroe used this research to map various states of consciousness, and to train others to alter their own consciousness at will. And the technology he helped create is today being used in a wide variety of fields, from health and medicine to higher learning.

Robert Monroe left his body for the last time on St. Patrick's Day 1995. He hadn't yet determined the source of the beam of light that triggered his astral career, nor the identities of the spiritual entities who assisted and guided him, though he suspected that one of these entities was himself, from far in the future. But his experiences, research, and writings have enlarged our understanding of our spiritual nature, and of the universe in which we live. They also offer a plausible explanation of our purpose here on earth, while providing an intriguing map and bridge to realms beyond the body.

VISION POWERS OF TUNKASHILA

Among all the peoples on earth, Native Americans are perhaps best known for their spiritual democracy. For they know that any person, young or old, can receive visions and guidance from the Great Spirit — referred to by some tribes as Tunkashila — the one who created and inhabits earth and sky, thunder and lightning, wind and rain, and pervades all living things. In the tribal tradition, a young brave would venture alone into the wilderness to fast and pray until he received a sacred vision by which he might live. The greatest warriors, healers, and shamans were those to whom great visions were given. The power of Tunkashila, it is said, pours through these great ones like abundant rain.

So it was with Black Elk, the Oglala Sioux warrior, healer, and shaman. Born in 1863 — a sad time for Native Americans, who were losing ground in their battle against the ever-encroaching white race — Black Elk grew up still hopeful that his people might survive as a great nation. From the beginning, his life was colored by the wrenching violence of the era. The Battle of a Hundred Slain, a Sioux victory over the white soldiers that crippled his father, was one of his earliest memories: "I remember that Winter of the Hundred Slain as a man might remember a bad dream," he later recalled. "It is like some fearful thing in a fog, a time when everything seemed troubled and afraid."

By the age of four, Black Elk first began to hear spirit voices calling him. When he was five, while riding his horse in the woods, he met his spirit guides:

I looked up at the clouds and two men were coming there, headfirst like arrows slanting down; and as they came they sang a sacred song and the thunder was like drumming. "Behold," they sang, "a sacred voice is calling you; all over the sky, a sacred voice is calling."

Over the next four years, in this time of change, Black Elk continued to hear the voices calling to him from time to time, but he did not understand what they wanted from him. Then, in his ninth year, while eating in a teepee, a voice spoke to him loud and clear, saying, "It is time; now they are calling you."

Black Elk went outside to look, but he saw nothing. Suddenly his legs began to hurt; the next day he collapsed and became ill. As he lay in his teepee looking through the open flap at the sky, he saw the two men come down again like arrows from the clouds. Black Elk's first great vision had begun:

Each warrior now carried a long spear from which jagged lightning flashed. I went out to meet them, feeling light as a spirit. A cloud descended and lifted me into the air, where I was summoned before the six Grandfather Spirits. So I went in and stood before the six, and they looked older than men can ever be — old like hills, like stars.

These ancient sky warriors revealed to Black Elk many things about himself, his people, and their tragic future to come. They gave him gifts of power, among them a wooden cup of water in which he saw the sky, and a warrior's bow. The water was the water of life, whose power was the power to heal. The bow was a weapon of war, whose power was the power to destroy.

Black Elk then witnessed an apocalyptic vision that rivals in its mythic depth and complexity the great visions of the biblical prophets. It lasted for twelve days. When it ended he found himself standing on the plain, far from his village. He quickly walked home, entered his teepee, and saw his parents sitting beside a sick boy covered with a blanket. That boy, lying there, was Black Elk himself. In the next moment, he found himself back in his body, under the blanket.

After Black Elk had rejoined his earthly form, his vision shone strong in his mind: "I could see it all again and feel the meaning with a part of me like a strange power glowing in my body." Being only nine years old, he could not yet fully understand all that he had seen — its meaning would unfold over time — but this vision would remain imprinted in his memory and spirit for the rest of his life.

> Nothing I have ever seen with my eyes was so clear and bright
> as what my vision revealed; no words I have ever heard with my
> ears were like the words I heard. I did not have to remember these
> things; they have remembered themselves all these years . . . even
> now I know that more was shown to me than I can tell.

Haunted by all that he had seen, Black Elk spent much time in solitude, thinking of it. But he told no one: "I wanted to be alone; it seemed I no longer belonged to my people, but to the spirit world . . . I could not make myself eat much; and my father and mother thought that I was still sick, but I was not — only homesick for the place where I had been."

Black Elk was destined to become, like the visionary leaders before him, a warrior, shaman, and sacred healer of the Sioux Nation. While still a boy, he took part in the battle of Little Big Horn, where General Custer made his foolhardy charge on the Sioux. And as a young man he followed the great warrior Crazy Horse, the holy warrior and hero who always charged into battle ahead of his warriors crying "Hoka hey! It is a good day to die!"

Crazy Horse had also received a great vision in childhood; in his case, he was given the power to fight like a spirit warrior whom arrows and bullets could not touch. His vision had given him the power to avoid all wounds in battle. His skin was never broken, even though he often led the charge where the white soldiers' bullets were thick as rain. Like many spirit-led souls, Crazy Horse did not fear death; he had foreseen in a vision the exact manner of his death, and met it bravely when it came.

Black Elk himself fought in many battles and healed many Sioux by the power that flowed through him. Some visions that foreshadowed what was to come were not of the spirit world but nightmarish events in this world: One of the first braves to arrive after the Wounded Knee Massacre, he found the bodies of several hundred of his tribe, mostly women and children, killed as they fled, scattered like dark patches in the white fields, slowly covered by flakes of falling snow.

"When I saw this," said Black Elk, "I wished I had died too."

At last the Sioux realized that the waves of white men would never end — that they would wash over the land, claiming it for their own and that the Sioux and other tribes would become like ghosts, their way of life snatched forever from their hands. But even when this world seemed senseless, the spiritual power of his childhood vision sustained Black Elk and gave him a sense of purpose and a reason for living. His visions and healing powers also gave strength to his people in this most tragic era.

Years later, he would tour Europe with Buffalo Bill's Wild West show and perform for Queen Victoria. In his heart he remained a shaman and a healer seeking to keep the old ways alive so that the spirit of his people might survive.

Near the end of his life Black Elk sometimes grieved, believing that he had failed to live up to his vision of preserving the sacred ways of his people. Even though he had the power to foresee many things, he did not see his own greatness, or know that he had accomplished his purpose. For by sharing his life in his spiritual autobiography — by revealing the visions that Tunkashila had granted him, Black Elk passed on knowledge that would help rekindle the American Indian Movement and generate a renaissance of Indian spirituality among generations of Americans. This great warrior, shaman, and healer fulfilled his divine destiny by helping to preserve forever — as long as the grass grows and the wind blows — the sacred ways and spirit of the Lakota Sioux.

AN UNLIKELY PILGRIM

One Woman's Twenty-Eight-Year Trek for Peace

Mildred Norman was born on a small New Jersey chicken farm in 1908. A review of her youth provides few clues to the destiny that lay ahead. Her family didn't attend church and adhered to no particular religion. Mildred graduated from high school, got a job, wore makeup, bought nice clothes, drove a fancy car, went out on dates, and wrote amateur plays for a local Grange group.

The momentum of conventional living carried Mildred into marriage just as America fell into the Great Depression of the 1930s. Her husband had trouble finding work, and later, due to differences in fundamental values, their paths eventually diverged and the marriage ended. In this time of crisis, Mildred began to question her entire existence and its meaning. It was a turning point and time of preparation for her life to come.

The seeds of her future were beginning to sprout; out of her inner search came new directions along the mountain paths she would hike — the solitude in the midst of nature's companionship brought clarity, as she prepared for something she couldn't yet name. In one six-month period, Mildred ended up hiking the entire length of the 2,050-mile Appalachian Trail — the first woman to do so.

Near the end of that journey came a revelation that was to shape the rest of her life. In her journal she wrote:

> *At the age of thirty, out of desperation, and a deep longing for*
> *a more meaningful way of life, while walking alone in the woods*
> *one night, I came to a moonlit glade and prayed. In that mo-*
> *ment, I felt a complete willingness, without any reservations, to*
> *give my life — to dedicate my life — to service. "Please use*
> *me!" I prayed to God. A great peace came over me.*

By morning's light, her old life was finished. But Mildred Norman's preparation had only begun.

Nothing in her early years had foreshadowed this transformation. Many family members, friends, and neighbors, dismayed by the changes in Mildred, dropped out of her life. What followed was fifteen years of testing — a war between what she called her "lower, self-centered nature and her higher, God-centered nature."

Struggling to integrate the spiritual awakening that came to her that night on her Appalachian journey, Mildred spent more and more time serving — working with senior citizens and the emotionally disturbed, and volunteering for various peace organizations. During this time, she slowly rid herself of unnecessary possessions, attachments, and useless activities. A pacifist and early advocate of voluntary simplicity, she pared her life to the bone. She now owned only two dresses — the second to wear while the other was in the wash.

Mildred's years of preparation culminated one morning in a second illumination, on her daily silent walk in nature:

> *All of a sudden I felt more uplifted than ever before — I knew*
> *timelessness, spacelessness, and lightness — I did not seem to*
> *be walking on the earth. Every bush, every tree seemed to wear*
> *a halo. . . . There was a light emanation around everything,*
> *and flecks of gold fell like slanted rain through the air. The*

*most important part was not the phenomena . . . it was the real-
ization of the unity of all creation.*

With this realization, the preparatory phase of Mildred's life
ended, and a new life began. She changed her name to Peace Pilgrim and resolved to walk across the length and breadth of North
America, speaking of peace among nations, of peace between individuals, and of the all-important inner peace.

Her life became a pilgrimage.

In the years that followed, Peace Pilgrim divested herself of all
possessions except for the clothes on her back — she kept no coat,
no sleeping bag, no money — only plain, rubber-soled shoes, long
pants, and a simple tunic. In her pockets she carried her only
earthly belongings: a folding toothbrush, a comb, a map of the area
where she was walking, and her current mail. She wore the tunic
over a long-sleeved shirt in winter, and short sleeves in the summer. On the back of her tunic, Peace Pilgrim had printed the
words, "10,000 miles for Peace." Later it changed to "25,000 miles"
— a number she far surpassed in her twenty-eight year pilgrimage,
in which she crossed each Canadian province once and the entire
United States nearly seven times.

As a pilgrim, Peace, as she was called, relied on the goodness
and generosity of others, and on the grace of God. She never asked
for food or lodging, but ate only what others offered freely. She
took her rest in country fields, parks, bus stations, and homes
across North America. Everywhere she walked she spoke of peace,
inspiring her listeners to consider their highest ideals, and to begin
or to continue living them.

Peace walked south in winter and north in summer; she had
her share of sweltering days, frozen nights, and mortal dangers.
But her faith in divine providence sustained her. When a hulking,
half-crazed teenage boy attacked her, she made no effort to defend

herself. She showed him only love and compassion, and was soon reassuring this lost young man that there was a way for him to find inner peace. Eventually he did. Another time a man invited her into his car, they talked a while, and he invited her to get some sleep. She curled up trustingly and did just that. When she awoke several hours later, he confessed to her that he'd planned to rape her, but her trust rendered him unable to go through with it.

Once she faced down another disturbed man attempting to assault an eight-year-old girl. Peace stood her ground, gazing at him without anger or criticism, until he finally turned and left. Peace often said, "There is a spark of good in everyone, no matter how deeply it may be buried. It is the real you." It was this divine spark that she addressed in every person she met.

Once, on an isolated road, Peace was caught by a sudden snow-storm — a blizzard so dense and fierce that she could not even see her hand in front of her face. Close to freezing, she surrendered to God's will and stumbled on. Soon she found the railing of a bridge. Groping her way down the snowy embankment, she crawled underneath the bridge and found a cardboard box filled with wrapping paper. She curled up inside it, and went to sleep.

Peace woke to a blue sky and sparkling sun. Another day had begun.

"Aren't people *good*!" she loved to say. And everywhere she went, people proved her right, opening their hearts and their hearths to her. In this way, for nearly three decades, Peace Pilgrim lived as a spiritual servant in the world, touching and inspiring thousands on her journey for peace. Today, she is known by millions worldwide for her simple yet profound message: "This is the way of peace: Overcome evil with good, falsehood with truth, and hatred with love. Live according to your highest light, and more light shall be given."

MODERN MAN OF MIRACLES

The Healing Powers of Padre Pio

After Therese Neumann, Padre Pio is perhaps the most widely observed modern Western mystic to demonstrate divine powers of healing and regeneration. The first signs of his extraordinary qualities occurred unexpectedly on September 20, 1918. Then a thirty-one-year-old Capuchin monk, Padre Pio was sitting alone in the monastery chapel, praying after Mass. Outside, Padre Leone heard a scream within the chapel and ran in to find Padre Pio lying unconscious on the floor, bleeding profusely from the five wounds of the stigmata.

Several monks carried Padre Pio to his room, where he begged them to keep his condition a secret. But word spread. The church quickly put a ban of silence on him, concerned that this untested monk might be manifesting symptoms of hysteria. He was forbidden to write or speak in public — yet over the next five decades, Padre would prove to be one of the most remarkable Western saints in history.

Like Therese Neumann, Padre Pio bore for his entire life wounds of the stigmata that never healed. And thousands of individuals — from ordinary Italian peasants and fellow clerics, to high public officials and pilgrims from around the world — witnessed and testified to his powers of telepathy, prophecy, bilocation, levitation, and healing.

Although Padre Pio never left the city of San Giovanni Rotondo in his last fifty years, he often appeared to those in need far from his physical body — to teach, admonish, comfort, and heal. Numerous testimonies, by telegram, letter, telephone transcript, and personal declaration, document Padre Pio's long-distance appearances in places he never physically visited — throughout Italy, Austria, Uruguay, and even Milwaukee, Wisconsin, where Padre Pio admitted appearing on June 25, 1950, to attend the death of a fellow monk's father. When asked about his ability to appear in two places, Padre Pio replied, "If Christ multiplied the loaves and fishes, why cannot he multiply me?"

And the fragrance of violets that often emanated from Padre Pio also often manifested to those who prayed to him, and was noticed by witnesses in those places where he had miraculously appeared.

Padre Pio's miraculous healing powers were well documented. He cured many illnesses deemed incurable, and on more than one occasion restored sight to the blind. His most well-documented case of healing involved a little blind girl named Gemma Di Giorgi, from Ribera, Sicily, who had been born with no pupils in her eyes. In 1947 her grandmother brought her on a long journey to see Padre Pio. Gemma's grandmother, ardently devoted to Padre Pio, believed the saint could give sight to her granddaughter, even though her doctors declared it physically impossible for a human being to ever see without pupils.

That morning, Gemma and her grandmother arrived in Padre Pio's village to wait in the enormous crowds that always attended

Padre Pio's Mass. Afterward, in the silence following Mass, all present heard a voice shout, "Gemma, come here!" Gemma's grandmother led her through the crowd up to Padre Pio, where they both knelt at his feet. Padre Pio, after hearing Gemma's confession, sweetly administered her first Communion, then gently stroked her eyes. Before they left, Padre Pio bid them farewell, saying, "May the Madonna bless you, Gemma. Be a good girl."

At that very moment, before the crowd of witnesses, Gemma uttered a shriek as the power of sight was given to her for the first time — a miracle that would last for the rest of her long life. Numerous doctors who examined Gemma later admitted their bewilderment. By all known science, she should not have been able to see without the apparatus required for sight.

The testimonies of miraculous cures and demonstrations of Padre Pio's supernatural abilities fill volumes. And the volumes written about this great contemporary saint are increasing each year.

Padre Pio left his body in 1968. More than one hundred thousand people came from around the world to attend his funeral in San Giovanni Rotondo, Italy, and half a million devotees would gather in Rome in 2002 to witness Pope John Paul II proclaim Padre Pio Saint Pio of Pietrelcina.

Many thousands wept at the passing of this humble saint, for the awe with which he was regarded for his miraculous powers was less than the love that his kindness had awakened in the hearts of his people.

THE FREEDOM WITHIN

A Healing Vision on the African Plain

In 1956, at the age of four, Malidoma Patrice Somé was kidnapped from his family and village by a French Jesuit missionary. With West Africa under French occupation, the Jesuits kidnapped many such children, hoping to raise an army of native missionaries to convert the African people from their tribal traditions to Christianity. Malidoma would spend the next fifteen years in captivity, indoctrinated by the Jesuits to be a priest.

The day of his kidnapping, Malidoma was taken to a Jesuit mission and locked in a concrete room with a metal door. When he protested, a missionary whipped the frightened boy until he collapsed unconscious on the floor. He awoke weeping for his mother. The beating taught Malidoma the consequences of protest and made him obedient as a slave.

At twelve he was sent to a large boarding school, a stone and concrete fortress housing over five hundred boys aged twelve to twenty-one. They were taught to speak French and forbidden to speak their native tongues. By then, few of the boys could remember their tribes or families, whom they learned were "damned and degraded beings living in sin."

The stick and the strap were often-used teaching tools. In time the cruelty of the missionaries made the boys cruel to one another. Dormitory life, with its numerous bullies and sexual predators, was a hellish realm. Younger, weaker boys were routinely molested. And Malidoma was molested by one of the missionaries. Over time, this brutality destroyed his faith. Once, when he was nearly drowned in a river by an older student, Malidoma tried praying to the God of these missionaries. But, he said, "It was like praying to the same one who had caused my misfortune."

At twenty, Malidoma fled from the boarding school into the jungle, rejecting the role of priest for which he had been groomed. He couldn't imagine luring his forgotten family and tribe into a religion that had caused him so much suffering. He walked for eleven days along the dusty roads and slept under trees and in the bush. Finally, dirty, starving, and exhausted, he reached Dano, the village where he was born. He managed to locate his old home. Finding no one there, he sat down under a nearby *nim* tree and fell asleep.

Malidoma awoke surrounded by curious children. Soon a young woman passed by, entered the house, came out to give him a drink, then went back inside — brother and sister did not recognize each other. Then a frail old man arrived on a bicycle; they exchanged greetings, looked curiously at each other, and the old man went inside — father and son did not recognize each other.

Finally an old woman walked up with a bundle of wood on her head. She looked at Malidoma strangely, came near him and hovered, and regarded him intensely. She walked forward and backward, engaged in inner struggle, looking back and forth from the river to Malidoma. Then, dropping her bundle of wood to the ground, she screamed, "Malidoma! Patrere! Malidoma!"

Recognizing her beloved son, Malidoma's mother rushed and knelt before him. She grabbed his hands and, with tears streaming down her face, began wailing, her grief mixed with joy.

Now Malidoma recognized his mother, and they wept together.

Malidoma's unexpected arrival produced a crisis in his family and his village. He had returned to his people as a stranger raised by their oppressors, no longer one of them. He did not speak their language or understand their customs. But slowly, as he had once learned a foreign tongue and Jesuit ways, Malidoma began to relearn Dagara, his forgotten native language. Within six months he could speak it passably well. His foreign education also proved useful — he could write letters for villagers to family members in faraway places. But he still felt lost, drifting between two worlds with no firm foothold in either one. His despair and alienation only intensified his wish to belong.

As his anguish reached a crisis, the village elders proposed a solution: To find his spirit and rejoin his people, Malidoma must undergo the Dagara tribal initiation, a dangerous, sometimes fatal ordeal. Dagara initiation expanded the subject's awareness beyond the ego or separate self — beyond the ordinary world — allowing the initiate to merge his own spirit with the universe of cosmic forces. The ordeal could open a doorway to another world hidden in everyday life. But initiates passed through this doorway only by confronting Terror and Death, which guard the portal to the spirit world.

The morning came when Malidoma and sixty-three youths from five villages went with their families to the edge of the bush. They stripped off their clothes and said good-bye to their families, knowing they might never see them again. Then, naked and singing, they followed the elders into the trees. Many hours later they arrived at a secluded spot in the savanna.

The six-week initiation involved prolonged periods of singing, dancing, fasting, meditation, and instruction by the elders, who terrified and dazzled the youths with their displays of shamanic power. These rituals and ordeals, which included spending one night standing buried up to their necks in a pit, opened doors to the "other world." Malidoma's first vision, vividly described in his memoir, *Of Water and the Spirit*, came after meditating nearly two days on a *yila* tree:

> *Out of nowhere, in the place where the tree had stood, appeared a tall woman — an extremely beautiful and powerful entity. I could sense the intensity emanating from her — an irresistible magnetic pull — she lifted her veil, revealing an unearthly face. She was green, light green. Even her eyes were green, though very small and luminescent. She was smiling and her teeth were the color of violet and had light emanating from them. The greenness in her had nothing to do with the color of her skin. She was green from the inside out, as if her body were filled with green fluid — her greenness was the expression of immeasurable love.*
>
> *Never before had I felt so much love — a love that surpassed any known classifications — we dashed toward each other and flung ourselves into each other's arms.... While she held me in her embrace, the green lady spoke to me for a long time in the softest voice that ever was — I cried abundantly...not because what she told me was sad, but because every word produced an indescribable sensation of nostalgia and longing in me.*

Hours later, healed and restored, Malidoma awoke from his vision to find himself hugging the *yila* tree. In a form he intuitively understood, the spirit world, in maternal guise, had given him a vision of cosmic love. Such experiences, far beyond his normal state of awareness, baffled him. Later one of the elders counseled him, "You do not need to understand everything right away. You have the rest of your life to comprehend what occurred. So be patient. Be happy you did not stay behind." He was referring to the four youths who had died during the initiation.

Malidoma told of another vision, and the realization it left him with long after its light had faded:

> *Slowly, like the dawn breaking, I began to see light . . . like an aurora borealis, shot through with areas of dark and ones of extreme luminescence — the light was so powerful that it would have fried my sight into blindness under ordinary circumstances, but somehow I was able to gaze at the skies of the underworld and survive. In that moment I saw that the light we encounter on the road to death is our own being, coming home to itself. This light is our own natural and eternal state.*

Malidoma's extraordinary experiences triggered a wholesale reorganization of his psyche, cleansing him of much confusion and healing him of deep wounds acquired through his bitter life experience. For the first time in fifteen years he was no longer an exile. He had come home at last.

Malidoma Patrice Somé went on to share with the West his story of exile and return, and the richness of his culture that imbues everyday life with spiritual meaning and presence. His story reveals that, in a sense, we have all been held captive, cut off from the spirit world and the wisdom of our ancestors. Like Malidoma, we each confront our own initiations that test us, teach us, and guide us home.

THE POWER OF LOVE

Saving Grace in the Dutch Underground

Jack Schwarz, born in Dordrecht, Holland, later emigrated to the United States to establish himself as a pioneer and expert in the fields of holistic self-health and human energy systems. He achieved worldwide recognition for his demonstrated ability to voluntarily control and regulate his body's so-called involuntary functions, such as pain, bleeding, breathing, heart rate — all documented in various scientific studies by Dr. Elmer Green of the Menninger Foundation, and other independent medical laboratories.

Also, as his wife Lois and close friends testified, Jack lived for many years eating only two or three small meals per week, and sleeping less than two hours a night while maintaining his abundant energy and busy schedule.

Jack's first initiations into the world of energetic healing abilities came at age nine, when he hugged his ailing mother, then ill with tuberculosis. After this simple embrace, she began to recover with unusual rapidity, and insisted that Jack's touch was the cause. Whether or not her perception was accurate, this incident created in Jack a curiosity about energy and healing, and opened his mind to the idea that such things might be possible, and that such unusual abilities might exist within himself.

A few years later, while working in a clothing store as a window dresser, Jack would routinely stick many straight pins into his lapel to keep them handy as he pinned outfits on the window models. One day a friend came up behind him, reached around, and gave Jack a playful but forceful slap on the chest — accidentally driving the pins deeply into Jack's flesh. Jack went to the washroom, pulled the pins out one by one, looked at his bleeding chest, and willed the bleeding and pain to cease. Both stopped immediately.

Excited by this discovery, Jack began experimenting on himself, deliberately piercing his own body with pins — and later with large knitting needles. He found that he was able to control both pain and bleeding. As time passed, Jack discovered he could also consciously accelerate the healing time of cuts and wounds, and resist infections as well.

But years before he became renowned for such abilities, Jack faced a life-and-death challenge — and experienced an intervention that pointed to a bridge between worlds, revealing to him the greatest power of all.

In 1940 the shadow of Nazi storm troopers spread across the face of Europe. When the war broke out, Jack, then sixteen, became a member of the Dutch underground. When the Nazis took over Jack's hometown of Dordrecht, they confiscated, as usual, the census records in order to learn the location of all able-bodied young men who were to be sent to work in slave-labor camps.

When the storm troopers came to the Schwarz household, the family hid Jack behind a false chimney. But after a careful search, the soldiers found him and took him to a railroad station, to wait for the train that would carry him to the labor camp. The next morning, before boarding the train, Jack saw his father, a small man, risking his life as he pushed his way through the masses of people and past the Nazi guards, to bring Jack his suitcase. He later wrote, "This was the first time I realized how much my father loved me."

Ironically, while the train was on the way to the labor camp in Hamburg, the Allies fired upon the tracks; many of the young men were injured, and some near Jack were killed. On arriving at the labor camp, word got out, perhaps through an informer, that Jack was a member of the Dutch underground. He was taken to a bare room for interrogation. There, a Nazi guard tied him up, tore off his shirt, and began whipping him with a cat-o'-nine-tails, flaying the skin from his back.

Jack, already adept at self-hypnosis, had by then taught himself to control his bleeding and dissociate his mind from physical pain. Being young, proud, and cocky, he first thought he would "show them." But the prolonged whipping was too much, and he finally fainted.

While unconscious, Jack experienced a profound vision — far more vivid than his waking life or his dreams: He found himself standing in a crowd of faceless people, before Christ on the cross. With his face full of love and agony, Christ looked down at them and said, "My God, why hast thou forsaken me?" In Jack's vision, Christ spoke not to God, but to the people in the crowd, and to Jack himself. In that moment, Jack knew he was being called to live Christ's way of love. He also understood that all human beings were actors playing their roles perfectly in a kind of world theater.

The consequences of his visionary realization were immediate:

Jack returned to consciousness filled with love and compassion for all. As the guard began to whip him again, Jack turned his head, looked into the guard's eyes, and said in German, "I love you."

He meant it with all his heart.

Dumbfounded, the Nazi dropped his whip and ran from the room. Later, another soldier took Jack back to his cell. He was left alone after that. Several months later, to his amazement, Jack was sent to Holland on an assigned task, apparently with the expectation that he would return voluntarily. Jack wholeheartedly accepted this opportunity to escape, and remained in Holland, serving in the Dutch underground until the war's end.

Years after the war, Jack emigrated to America.

In 1958, Jack Schwarz founded the Aletheia Foundation in Mendocino, California, where, for more than forty years, until his passing, he helped men and women of all ages explore and develop their own capacities for healing, regeneration, and self-discovery.

AWAKENED TO HEAL

Internal Energy Creates a New Life Purpose

For years now, the Chinese government has studied unique individuals with a variety of extraordinary powers. They are called *special ability people*. Some of them have developed their remarkable abilities through advanced internal energy practices called Chi Gong. Others, however, have acquired their powers spontaneously, by mysterious means.

Mei Mei Xiang is an example of one such person.

Before moving to Beijing, Mei, an elementary schoolteacher, lived in Northeast China with her husband and son. A modest person, she was well liked by her students and neighbors. One afternoon in the mid-1980s, Mei rode her bicycle into the city to attend an annual fair, a traditional celebration honoring the ancestors. There was music, food, dancing, and people in colorful costumes dressed as heavenly spirits, ancestors, and historical figures.

Riding home afterward, Mei grew tired and stopped for a short nap at the foot of Lady Mountain, known for centuries by locals as an abode of the goddess Quan Yin. Mei arrived home after dark. That same night she experienced sudden and severe stomach cramps. The next day when they grew worse, she feared it was food poisoning from the fair. She was about to go to the hospital when the cramps suddenly stopped; a strange rushing force filled her belly, then flooded her body. Her skin tingled with electricity. She felt feather light, and exhilarated.

The force lifted her up; she found herself walking effortlessly on her toes in an intoxicated state, then dancing giddily around her house. To release the storm of energy that threatened to overwhelm her, she went out and began to walk, then dance, still on her toes, across a field, into the streets, even through traffic. Mei ran and skipped down the crowded sidewalk without bumping into anyone, feeling weightless, guided with unerring precision by the powerful force. She felt her body both absorbing and radiating energy.

Every day after that, waves of energy flooded through her in cycles, building to an almost unbearable intensity, at which point she was compelled to release it through vigorous movements and dancing. Her friends, family, and neighbors grew puzzled and worried about her. Many thought she had gone mad. Mei herself did not understand what was happening. But she felt extremely clear, happy, and energetic. Although at times she feared being overwhelmed by the intense energies flooding through her, she sensed that something important was happening to her, and intuitively trusted what was occurring.

This process lasted one hundred days and was accompanied by states of exultation, as she heard inner voices and witnessed remarkable visions and fantasies. Mei felt she was in contact with the spiritual world. On the hundredth day, Mei prepared fruit and food and told her husband, "Today everyone is here: Buddha, Quan Yin, the Heavenly Emperor and Heavenly Mother. I must prepare food for our guests." For the first time since her experience had begun, Mei felt emotionally and psychologically stable — able to contain the energy flowing through her. Her fears of being overwhelmed by the force began to subside.

At this point, the force began producing new phenomena. Now she heard ancient music that sent her into deep trances, or moved her into ecstatic states as she began to dance. Many people who saw her found her dancing eerie, yet beautiful to watch. Mei also found she could now look into people's bone structure and see the energy flow in their bodies. On other occasions, she could see faraway people or events. And her hands were charged with electrical energy; once on the bus she grabbed the metal handrail and everyone suddenly let go, some crying out from the shock. She could sometimes open locks simply by touching them.

When Mei went out in public she often heard a cacophony of people's thoughts crowding in on her, or saw images, symbols, and nonphysical entities, even fairy-tale and mythic characters from ancient times. At other times she was overwhelmed by information pouring through her too rapidly to process, as if an inner floodgate of knowledge had opened within her. Mei described this period:

> *At that time I traveled many places in my mind — sometimes I was on top of a mountain; other times I was underwater, or in a different city. I often felt confused, but a voice was always with me, reassuring me. Every day I went to the park to dance to the music only I could hear. I had to do this to survive my strange experience.*

One day while cooking meat for her family, a voice told Mei, "You cannot eat this food." After that she could not eat killed flesh. When she saw a piece of meat she saw the creature as it had been in its living form.

Then one evening, the voice told her, "It's time for you to heal people and serve society." So Mei began a new experiment with the energy flowing through her, to see if she could use it to heal. She found that when she stood before a sick person and thought "I want to heal this person," her hands raised automatically to massage the air inches from the place in their bodies that needed healing. She felt energy pour through her into them, and many reported that their pains and ailments disappeared.

Initially, Mei's strange behavior had made her well known as "the teacher who went crazy." Soon she became famous throughout her city as a healer. As she came to better understand the principles and methods she had applied spontaneously, she began teaching others to heal. Eventually, she moved to Beijing and opened a Chi Gong clinic and school for healers. Mei's "religious" ideas were officially frowned on by the Communist party. Yet she reported that many party officials had come to see her privately.

Mei called her art Yu Zhou Zi Ran Gong, or "Skill of Universal Nature." Having learned to control and conduct what at first was an overwhelming flood, she tapped into this Universal Nature to access information and energy. Mei has continued to pursue her calling, first awakened by her experiences with internal energy. She has said that the spirit-energy called Chi is unlimited, existing everywhere and in everything; when the channels of our mind and body open, it pours through us to heal and balance our being and awaken our higher human capacities.

KINGDOM OF COMPASSION

A Warrior Becomes a Buddha

More than three hundred years before the birth of Christ, the invincible armies of Alexander stormed across the ancient world. But Alexander's dreams of world conquest died on the shores of the Ganges — the river he would never cross. Two years later, another great warrior rose from obscurity to conquer the same territory that had defeated Alexander the Great. The warrior's name was Maurya, and his ever-expanding kingdom, the Mauryian Empire, would come to be known as India.

As the years passed, Maurya's kingdom passed to his son, Bindusara, then to his grandson, Asoka, a battle-hardened warrior whose driving ambition rivaled that of Alexander. King Asoka spent his early years at war, conquering his neighboring provinces. Then, in the eighth year of his forty-year reign, Asoka defeated the nation of Kalinga — a staggering victory in which one hundred thousand Kalingans were slain and one hundred and fifty thousand were taken captive. Many thousands of Asoka's own men died, and thousands of wounded on both sides perished in the days that followed.

Kalinga was now Asoka's. Yet his moment of supreme triumph

produced an unprecedented and wholly unpredictable result: As Emperor Asoka gazed upon the field of slaughter, contemplating its godlike harvest of dead, he was overcome by a grief and remorse that changed not only his life, but the future of India.

In that moment of profound mourning, Asoka understood the value of all living things, the primal horror of war, and the petty hunger for earthly glory that had lured him to this act of supreme folly. The revelations that came to him on that corpse-laden plain forever seared his soul, opened his eyes and heart, and released in his mind a ray of light seen in few kings before or since.

It was Asoka's last battle. That day he renounced forever the use of war as a tool of state. He now understood the sole task worthy of a true emperor: to influence his subjects by his own example — by ruling with justice and mercy, and living with love. Asoka devoted the rest of his life to this end. He wrote:

> When a country is conquered, people are killed, they die, or are made captive. Thus arose His Sacred Majesty's remorse for having conquered the Kalingas. . . . Today, if a hundredth or a thousandth part of those who suffered in Kalinga were to be killed, to die, or to be taken captive, it would be grievous to His Sacred Majesty. . . . If anyone does him wrong it will be forgiven as far as it can be forgiven. . . . For His Sacred Majesty desires safety, self-control, justice, and happiness for all beings.

Asoka embodied these words in ten thousand noble deeds, which he performed over the next thirty-three years of his extraordinary reign. In the classic memoir *Autobiography of a Yogi*, Paramahansa Yogananda relates just a few of the deeds that made Asoka among the greatest kings India, and perhaps the world, has ever seen:

Emperor Asoka erected 84,000 religious stupas [shrines] in various parts of India. Fourteen rock edicts and ten stone pillars survive. Each pillar is a triumph of engineering, architecture, and sculpture. He arranged for the construction of many reservoirs, dams, and irrigation sluices; of highways and tree-shaded roads dotted with rest houses for travelers; of botanical gardens for medicinal purposes; and of hospitals for man and beast.

The effects of Asoka's divine realization — like the sermons carved in stone through which he preached his message of compassionate justice — spread across his vast empire and down through the centuries. Even today, although little known outside of India, Asoka's transformation continues to influence our world.

Asoka's championing of Buddhism, then barely two centuries old, helped this fledgling religion flourish and spread to become one of the great world religions. By outlawing the killing of animals for sport and making ahimsa — noninjury — his national policy, Asoka fostered nonviolence as a religious principle among India's many faiths, and spread philosophically based vegetarianism throughout Indian culture, and from India to the Western world, where it continues to blossom today.

To establish compassionate justice as the foundation of his kingdom, Asoka ended the use of torture, which his warrior-grandfather Maurya had honed to barbaric perfection. Asoka also created and sent to every province a multitude of new public officials called Officers of Righteousness. Their sole mission was to prevent wrongful punishment and imprisonment, and to promote "welfare and happiness among servants and masters, Brahmans and the rich, the needy and the aged."

Remarkably, every soldier in his vast army was instructed in the Golden Rule — that we must treat others as we wish to be treated. This principle Asoka called the Law of Life. Even when defending his kingdom from invaders, Asoka used force only as a last resort, when moral reasoning and peaceful negotiation had failed.

His example has inspired countless Indian men and women through the ages, including Mahatma Gandhi, Jawaharlal Nehru, India's first prime minister, and Nehru's daughter, Indira Gandhi, India's first woman prime minister. Though himself a Buddhist, Asoka preached universal tolerance among all religions. He inscribed on his instructive monuments, "All sects deserve reverence for one reason or another. By thus acting a man exalts his own sect and at the same time does service to the sects of other people." Asoka further demonstrated a deep support for the integrity of all religions by ordering his Officers of Righteousness to defrock all monks, even Buddhists, who failed to live the tenets of their faith, setting high standards still relevant and needed today.

Such was the glory of Emperor Asoka, who began his career as a warrior, was converted by despair and illumination on the field of battle, and won his greatest spiritual victory by making himself a servant to the needs of his people. Asoka's supreme embodiment of the universal principles he taught marks him as a true bodhisattva — a Buddhist saint — and a visionary of the past, present, and future, whose light can guide today's leaders into the new millennium.

MADONNA IN LIGHT

Seeing Is Believing

On the eve of America's Roaring Twenties, in twentieth-century Zeitoun, a suburb of Cairo, Egypt, a wealthy and devout Muslim donated a piece of land to the city for the purpose of building a Christian church. What made his donation even more unusual was that he stated that he had been directed to do so by the Virgin Mary, who had appeared to him in a particularly vivid dream. Five years later, with the church completed, Mary again visited the Zeitoun man in a dream and promised to appear in the church the following year.

If Mary did appear as promised, she was not seen by anyone who reported it.

Forty-three years passed; the devout old Muslim and his prophetic dream were by then forgotten — until the night of April 2, 1968. Two Muslim mechanics working late in the auto repair shop across from St. Mary's Church of Zeitoun went out for some fresh air. Looking up, they saw a glowing female figure standing on the church top by the central dome. Confused, they first thought the woman was a nun contemplating suicide. One of the mechanics ran to fetch the church pastor, while the other called an emergency squad.

When they returned, the figure was gone.

Others must have also seen the figure, for word quickly spread that a luminous lady had appeared on the church. Small crowds began to gather each night, waiting expectantly for her return.

One week later, on April 9, the woman reappeared, emanating an aura of white light — this time before a small gathering. From then on, her brightly glowing figure, clothed in flowing robes of light, appeared randomly and frequently on the church's roof at night. Word-of-mouth and news reports spread the story, and the crowds grew. It was not long before photographs of startling clarity captured the unearthly visitor.

The apparition, whom many believed to be Mary, manifested dozens of times in the first two months, with each appearance lasting from ten minutes to several hours. These appearances weren't merely a local event covered in the back pages of the town newspapers; the city had to tear down several old nearby buildings to accommodate the crowds that gathered nightly, often numbering in the tens of thousands, and at times reaching one hundred thousand.

One remarkable aspect of this phenomenon was its dazzling and varied displays of light. Before Mary's arrivals, bright flashes played about the cathedral or plummeted cometlike from the sky. In sudden bursts of radiance, "doves of light" fluttered about the dome or soared far out over the city. Radiant stars at times surrounded the apparition. On other occasions, the entire dome was illumined; one witness described it as "engulfed in a brilliant blue white light, as if it were melting . . . the edges of light on top of the lighted dome appeared to roll inward so that one's eyes were directed to the very center."

These phenomena were extensively witnessed, photographed, and documented. Bishop Samuel, official investigator for the Coptic Christian Church, witnessed the apparition numerous times and filed a detailed report. Deeply moved by his experiences, he wrote: "The scene was overwhelming and magnificent. The apparition walked toward the west, sometimes moving its hands in blessing and sometimes bowing repeatedly. A halo of light surrounded its head. I saw some glittering beings around the apparition. They looked like stars."

Bishop Athanasius, sent by the Coptic Pope Kryllos VI to investigate and report on these appearances, was equally impressed. He wrote:

> There she was, five or six meters above the dome, high in the sky, full figure, like a phosphorous statue, but not so stiff as a statue. There was movement of the body and of the clothing. . . . One would estimate the crowd at 100,000. . . . Our Lady looked to the north; she waved her hand; she blessed the people, sometimes in the direction where we stood. Her garments swayed in the wind. She was very quiet, full of glory. It was something really supernatural, very, very heavenly.

The "lady of light" made hundreds of appearances over a period of two years, and finally disappeared in 1971. All told, hundreds of thousands witnessed the apparition; numerous photographic records exist, with detailed testimonials by news reporters, church officials, and thousands of citizens of different faiths and social position. Although the precise nature of these visitations remains unknown, their reality is well documented.

Our conventional assumptions about the nature of reality, and about the kinds of beings that inhabit or appear in this world, are called into question and perhaps expanded by these sightings of an ethereal lady, bathed in light, on a church top in the Cairo district of Zeitoun.

ADVERSITY'S TEACHER

Prison Camp Hardship to Heroic Service

Young Afrikaner Laurens van der Post's relationships with the Bushmen of the African veldt deeply influenced his values, character, and destiny in the early part of the twentieth century. The people of the bush nursed him, taught him, and befriended him, and he marveled at their intimate embrace of nature and their affinity with the world of spirits. He loved their tales of wonder and magic, and hungrily absorbed their perception of the world as a mythic realm where humans, confronted by mysterious powers, found stories that gave life meaning. He took to heart the importance of finding a defining story for himself, and resolved that he, too, would create his life out of his dreams.

A Bushman hunter once explained to young Laurens, "You see it is very difficult and unpredictable, because there is a dream dreaming us." Raised in the presence of such people and infused with their enchanting view of reality, it isn't surprising that van der Post's character blended realism and idealism, with a large dash of the heroic thrown in.

A farm boy later drawn to war, Laurens became a soldier for

ten years and led commando guerrilla units behind enemy lines in Abyssinia (Ethiopia), North Africa, and the Far East. At one point during World War II, Laurens and his men were captured by the Japanese and put in a concentration camp. There they entered into those extreme twilight depths the Bushmen call the Time of the Hyena — "a state of madness," Laurens wrote, "of unbearable tragedy... when not only the light of the mind was invaded by darkness, but life itself was overcast with the approach of... death."

The prisoners were starved and tortured and forced to watch their comrades executed for minor infractions. Yet in the midst of this madness Laurens also encountered the power that the Bushmen embraced as "the source of existence," and he confronted the mystery he had sensed in their way of being even as a child. He wrote:

> *Taken out to what we thought could be our own execution, we were made by the Japanese to watch the most brutal execution of others. During this forced spectacle, an officer standing between me and a friend called Nick fainted. . . . Nick and I supported him as he stood there; in the process we all touched hands. I was startled by this, because throughout my physical being there was an inrush of what I can only describe as electricity, which was not just a thing of energy, but was charged with a sense of hope, certainty, belonging, and life everlasting.*
>
> *I knew then — and the knowledge has since grown and not dimmed — that this is what flesh and blood is about and is meant to be. But for this illumination I do not know how I could have steered my course in the years that have followed ... the post-war human world appears stubbornly determined to deny and destroy that oneness of life we are meant to share.*

That sudden Promethean flash of spirit, ignited in the face of death, had far-reaching effects. Filmmaker Mickey Lemle described how Laurens spent his remaining years in the camp: "Laurens created a make-shift university... that at one point offered 144 courses a week. The prisoners wrote out textbooks on toilet paper, and after three and a half years, men matriculated and received diplomas, also written out on toilet paper."

"After the war," Laurens told Lemle, "six people armed with their toilet paper diplomas got jobs in the British foreign service."

Billy Griffiths, a fellow prisoner who had lost both hands and both eyes, credited Laurens with keeping him alive "when I no longer wanted to live. He would say to me, 'Hang on, Billy. Hang on. There is more to life than hands and eyes.' He was right."

They remained friends for nearly fifty years.

Like others before him, Laurens survived adversity and inhuman atrocity by finding light in the darkness and meaning in the madness. More than that, he found a way to share that meaning with his fellow prisoners, and with others in the world at large. Laurens's prison experience and awakening turned his life into an urgent quest for meaning, an inquiry into fundamental questions — a "continuous search after self-knowledge."

After the war his life came full circle, back to his childhood roots. Laurens was one of the first to recognize that the Bushmen he loved, and among whom he had been born and raised, faced extinction under European colonialism. He was also among the first to act: He began exploring hidden Africa, determined to "make one last effort to preserve the Bushman and his culture in the heart of what I called the lost world of the Kalahari, and try to arrest there, this age-old story of persecution and annihilation." Laurens persuaded the British government to help him in his task:

All I wanted was recognition of [the Bushmen's] humanity and his values that were at their best precious qualities that we had neglected in ourselves and at our peril; and his right to native land wherein his security was guaranteed so as to give him time enough to find a way of his own into the world of the future.

To this cause Laurens devoted much of his writings and his remaining years. His expeditions to the Kalahari Desert, and his prolonged heroic effort to save the Bushmen from extinction, produced numerous books and several documentaries, perhaps most famous among them *The Lost World of the Kalahari*.

Shortly before his death at the age of ninety, Sir Laurens van der Post shared the following insight with his friend Mickey Lemle: "Meaning transfigures all.... Once what you are living and what you are doing has meaning for you, it is irrelevant whether you are happy or unhappy. You're content. You're not alone in your spirit. You belong."

GRANDMOTHER'S GUIDANCE

A Dream That Spared Generations

Ever since she was a girl, Jean Munzer had known that she and her family owed their lives to a visitation that occurred in a dream to her mother, Clara. The incident, which took place before Jean was conceived, also involved Jean's grandmother, who at the time had been dead for more than twenty years.

Clara was born in Vienna, Austria, in the early 1900s. She never knew her mother, who had died while giving birth to her, or her father, who died of an infection a year later. Instead, Clara was raised by her maternal grandparents, who owned a prosperous store.

As a teenager, Clara worked in her grandparents' store. That's where fifteen-year-old Siegfried Gruen first saw her; he approached her and placed on the counter before her a book of poems he had written.

"I write poems too," Clara said.

So began a friendship and a lifelong romance that would last for more than sixty years.

During the three years after their first meeting, Clara and Siegi were inseparable. They pledged their love to each other despite her grandparents' disapproval. Their objections were conventional: They were prospering middle-class business folk, while Siegi came from a poor family. And Clara was too young. But no "reasons" could halt their blossoming love.

Even when Siegi — a singer, actor, and poet — went to America in his eighteenth year, he wrote Clara nearly every day, a practice he would continue for six years. He lived with his uncle in Michigan and worked in his uncle's shoe store. A gifted singer, he eventually sang in the Detroit Opera. But after fulfilling his dream of becoming a U.S. citizen, Siegi returned to Vienna to fulfill another more important dream: to marry Clara and bring her back with him to America.

But another obstacle presented itself; although Clara's grandparents had resigned themselves to her marrying Siegi, they wanted her to remain in Vienna, fearing that if she went to America they would never see her again. Clara herself did not want to leave Vienna or her grandparents, though she wanted to marry Siegi. So a solution was proposed: In order to keep Clara near, her grandparents offered to set Siegi up with his own business in Vienna. Clara fervently campaigned for this plan, and at last persuaded Siegi, who was willing to sacrifice his American dream for love. It seemed the matter was settled.

But on the night before Siegi was to sign the contract for his new business, Clara had an extraordinary dream: Her dead mother, whom she had never known, appeared vividly to Clara, and urgently told her that she must leave Vienna and go to America with her future husband. Clara was not given to psychic or paranormal experiences. Yet this dream seemed much more than a dream to her, and it affected her deeply. She awoke firmly convinced that her mother had in fact come to her for reasons beyond her understanding, to deliver a message of great importance and urgency. She knew that she must obey.

Early that morning Clara ran to Siegi's house and told him that he could not sign the business contract — that they must go to America together. Siegi, surprised by her sudden change of heart and the unusual event that prompted it, happily agreed. Clara and Siegi were married soon after, and when they emigrated to America, a number of Siegi's relatives went with them.

Several years later Hitler invaded Austria. Most of the members of Clara's and Siegi's families who remained in Vienna were taken to concentration camps, where many of them died.

Jean Munzer considered this story more than a family heirloom. Her mother's dream made her family's future possible, and influenced Jean's lifework:

> *My parents and my father's family who came to America were saved by my mother's dream. Myself, my children, their children, and all our future generations, owe our lives to a dream warning given to my mother, Clara, by my grandmother who had long before passed from this world.*

Jean further explained:

> *That dream was the first and only "psychic" experience that my mother would ever have. But what an important one it was for our family. My mother's story has illumined my life. It has shown me that other realities exist besides the one we see; that spiritual protection and guidance are available to us in this life and beyond; and that we can trust our inner wisdom in whatever form it comes.*

From 1978 until her passing, Jean Munzer served as the director of the Metaphysical Center of New Jersey. Well versed in the realities of different dimensions, she lectured throughout the world, and her work has been included in eight biographical references, including *Who's Who in the World* and *Foremost Women of the Twentieth Century*.

VOYAGER WITHIN

Jung's Courageous Journey into the Psyche

Carl Jung is best known as a renowned psychiatrist and author, an explorer of dreams and of human nature. Many also know him as the originator of a new psychology — one that embraced the soul and declared spirit as a living force at the center of the psyche. Yet few are aware that Jung's contributions resulted from his own extraordinary, often otherworldly experiences.

Born in Basel, Switzerland in 1875, Carl's character was deeply influenced by his father, a church pastor who had lost his faith. His sensitive temperament came more from his mother, an intuitive woman given to spontaneous outbursts of profound insight, around whom mysterious events seemed to happen: On one such occasion a solid oak table in front of her emitted a sound like a gunshot and split down the middle, against the grain; on another, a thick steel knife in a bread basket loudly exploded into neatly sheered fragments. Such events, which had no rational explanation, helped generate the first stirrings of Carl's inquiries into life's deeper realities.

Carl's destiny was also influenced by a rich internal world of vivid dreams and fantasies, and he would devote his entire life to exploring this inner realm of inexhaustible mysteries. "Man's psyche," he claimed, "is as infinite within as the universe is without."

Fascinated by the supernatural and the possibility of life beyond death, and curious about the human soul, Carl was drawn to an exciting new science called psychiatry, then in its infancy. After completing his doctorate he took a position in a mental hospital in Zurich, where each day he confronted the haunting specter of minds destroyed by every kind of madness.

Psychiatry at that time was mainly concerned with identifying, naming, and cataloging the various types of mental illness. Patients were regarded as merely pitiful objects to be studied — soulless wrecks from whose lives useful knowledge might be extracted. But Jung saw his patients as complex human beings, each containing a unique if hidden story, each guarding a mystery waiting to be discovered. Jung called this hidden story "the secret ... the rock against which he is shattered." He began to search for that story in all of his patients, convinced that it held the key to their healing.

Throwing himself passionately into his work, Carl delved into his patients' psyches, and his own, emphasizing the importance of the human relationship in the healing process. He believed a physician should not hide behind a mask of superiority. "A doctor is effective only when he is affected," Jung wrote. "Only the wounded physician heals."

The publication of Jung's first book brought him to the attention of another great man then making a name for himself: Sigmund Freud. The two began to correspond, each recognizing and respecting the other's genius. So began a professional and personal relationship marked by both fruitful collaboration and historic conflict.

Freud called Jung his "crown prince and heir." But Carl's mission lay waiting in his own uncharted depths. He felt compelled to uncover the spiritual implications of mental illness, while Freud dogmatically emphasized the sexual source of all psychological disturbances. To Freud the idea of spirit was a delusional construct masking sexual repression. But Carl considered spirit, or soul, the essential core of humanity's being. Their increasingly diverging visions would become irreconcilable.

Freud insisted that Carl's radical ideas were wrong, and dangerously close to mysticism. His increasing efforts to discourage Carl from pursuing his own vision forced Carl to choose between the embrace of a revered authority, father figure, and mentor, and the call of his own destiny. After long and agonized soul-searching, Carl chose the lonely path to greatness.

The split between Freud and Jung, when it came, plunged Carl into a state of profound uncertainty, self-doubt, and intellectual paralysis. Now shunned by most of the international psychiatric community, Carl lost his footing and felt himself falling into an abyss. His descent was marked by cataclysmic dreams and terrifying visions. In one he saw a rising flood submerge the European continent, destroying nations and drowning multitudes before turning into a sea of blood. (After World War I began the following year, he saw his vision as a premonition arising out of what he would later call the *collective unconscious*.)

At first Carl feared he might be going mad, perhaps entering a psychosis that would destroy him. Even so, as a dedicated scientist, he kept a journal of his inner process, thinking to leave a record behind so that at least some human knowledge might be salvaged from his destruction. For months he struggled against these inner visions and forces.

Finally Carl realized he had to explore the very shadows he most feared. If he lacked the courage to face his own demons, how could he ever hope to heal others? And so Carl Jung began a conscious, deliberate journey into the psychic underworld that would last for years — often a desperate, terrifying period full of apocalyptic visions, fears of madness, and spiritual encounters with the denizens of the heaven and hell within his own psyche. In the process of exploring this inner landscape, and struggling to understand all that he encountered in these inner depths and heights, he followed in the steps of another great scientist-shaman, Emanuel Swedenborg.

At his time of greatest peril, as his inner forces threatened to overwhelm him (Carl kept a loaded revolver in a drawer near his bed, and had considered suicide), an inner guide appeared to him — a wise old man who called himself Philemon. In long, internal conversations, Philemon counseled Carl, displaying profound and original insights that often surprised the psychiatrist. The scientist in Carl speculated that Philemon must be a facet of his own mind; yet the shaman within him related to Philemon as an independent and superior entity.

Carl wondered at the nature of this mysterious figure. Was Philemon merely an imaginary creation? Or something more mysterious? Jung came to understand that Philemon was both a part of his psyche *and* a being with an individuated existence of his own. Carl fully accepted this unique relationship and later referred to Philemon as his "guru," a guide on his journey through the unconscious. Whatever his ultimate nature, Philemon and the forces he represented transformed Carl Jung's relationship to psychiatry and to his own psyche — and perhaps saved his life. With Philemon's help, Jung the scholar and scientist passed through an inner abyss and crossed the shaman's bridge between worlds into the life of an illumined mystic. As a result of these years of inner work, Jung emerged as a prolific figure of great genius.

New energy, ideas, and insights came flooding through Carl. He began to write for the first time in nearly a decade. In time he would produce over thirty volumes of profound scope and depth — firsthand reports of a man who had traveled to the innermost regions of the psyche and returned with undreamed-of riches. Among these was an original psychiatric model of the mind that included the soul, and that viewed humanity's psychological processes in the light of our spiritual nature.

One night, in the second half of his life, Carl woke to see a greenish gold figure of a crucified Christ hovering over him, "marvelously beautiful," bathed in bright light. This central religious figure had a deep impact on Carl. Ever a scientist, he sought to grasp the meaning of this vision held within his psyche. He came to understand his vision of "the Christ" as an alchemical symbol of the union of spirit and matter in human flesh — that meeting of opposites we are called upon to integrate in order to become whole. Jung the scientist had provided keys to unlock the spiritual treasures of the world religions.

Carl's vision led him to study ancient alchemical texts. Before he cracked the code, alchemists were thought of as crude scientists, or magicians, seeking to change lead into gold. But Jung discovered that they were in fact a secret brotherhood of mystics driven underground by the inquisition, whose true goal was spiritual transmutation — changing the lead of unconsciousness into the gold of transcendent awareness. He found in these alchemical works clear confirmation of many of his psychological theories. His wide-ranging explorations resulted in the classic theories taught today in nearly every school of psychology and psychiatry worldwide.

At the age of sixty-nine, Carl Jung suffered a heart attack and found himself floating in space, a thousand miles above Earth, "bathed in blue light . . . the most glorious thing I had ever seen." In this vision — one of the most significant of his life — he landed on a black meteorite where "a black Hindu sat silently in lotus posture upon a stone bench" before the entrance to a temple. As he was about to enter the temple, Carl felt everything he had been, done, experienced, known, and accomplished — all his hopes, desires, and goals — stripped away from him, until only his essence remained.

Jung later wrote, in *Memories, Dreams, Reflections*: "I had the certainty I was about to enter an illumined room and . . . I would at last . . . know what had been before me, why I had come into being and where my life was flowing." But before he could enter, he saw his doctor rise up as a spirit from the earth, framed "by a golden laurel wreath." He had been sent to bring Carl back. The next instant, Jung found himself back in his body, sick at heart — he had longed to enter that temple where the riddle of his life would be solved.

During his weeks of recovery, Carl experienced a series of exalted visions: "These were states of ineffable joy. Angels were present, and light. . . . Night after night I floated in a state of purest bliss, 'thronged round with images of all creation.' " At this point the most productive period of his lifework began. "A good many of my principal works were written only then," he recalled. "Something else, too, came to me . . . an affirmation of things as they are: an unconditional 'yes' to that which is . . . acceptance of the conditions of existence . . . of my own nature."

Carl Jung died at the age of eighty-six, productive to the very end. His writings, born of his journey into the wilderness of the human psyche, mark him as one of the towering figures of our age. His life-changing encounters with the spiritual forces and entities he discovered there — forces at work and at war within each of us — have helped illuminate humanity's path to the spiritual treasures waiting as we cross the bridge to our own inner worlds.

ADDICT TO ARTIST

A Lost Soul Finds New Purpose

Andy Lakey was born in France in 1959 to a half Spanish, half French mother and an American father. His family later moved to Ohio, then Japan, then Kansas, and finally to California. Maybe it was the instability, or not fitting in — or maybe there was no particular reason at all —but by the time Andy graduated from high school and joined the Navy, drugs had become an integral part of his life. He didn't last long in the Navy, though he managed to leave with an honorable discharge.

Andy soon found a lucrative occupation as a car salesman. But as his career ascended, so did his drug use. Cocaine, which he smoked in a freebase pipe, was his drug of choice. By 1986, at the age of twenty-seven, Andy was making eighty-five thousand dollars a year, much of which went up in smoke — the highest quality cocaine money could buy. He was going nowhere, in the fast lane.

Then, on New Year's Eve, Andy Lakey received a wake-up call.

It came like a bolt of lightning. While greeting New Year's freebasing cocaine in a friend's apartment upstairs from his own, his heart suddenly began palpitating rapidly, and he felt extremely ill.

"I felt certain I was going to die," he said.

Staggering out of the room, Andy collapsed in the hall, then somehow stumbled downstairs to his apartment. Leaving the door open behind him, Andy got into the shower fully clothed and turned on the cold water, hoping it might revive him. With the water pouring over him, feeling frightened and alone, he bowed his head against the wall and prayed for the first time since he was eight years old.

"I still remember the prayer," he reported. "I said, 'God is good. God is great. God, if you let me live, I will never do drugs again'" — desperate words similar to those muttered by countless people down on their luck before him — but Andy meant it with all his heart. And he added, "I will also do something to help humankind." He further reported:

Almost instantly, I felt a twirling sensation, like a little tornado or whirlpool around my feet . . . there were seven figures, and as they twirled up toward my knees, my thighs, my waist and up to my chest, the twirling got faster and faster. . . . When they reached my heart, they came together as one and put their arms around me . . . now there was only one figure. . . . It embraced and lifted me into another dimension. There were a thousand planets with ten thousand poles of light extending through them and into . . . a galaxy of brightness. . . . Every pole was filled with millions of souls in perfect columns and perfect harmony. But I could not get into a pole.

At that point, Andy woke up in the emergency room — his friend had found him unconscious in the shower and brought him to the hospital just in time. The doctor told him that due to the massive amount of cocaine in his body, his heart had started to fail.

Andy woke up totally free of his years-long dependency on drugs.

This near-death lesson, with its staggering vision, was not lost on him. Andy vowed to change his life. He started by finding a new job, since most of his business acquaintances were also his party friends. Meanwhile, he began to contemplate the meaning of his vision — a vision he resolved to bring into this world — first by drawing it, then by painting it. This project became an obsession to which he devoted every spare moment, every night.

On his thirtieth birthday, Andy quit work to become a full-time artist. "The only problem," he related, "was that I had never learned how to paint." This small obstacle would not deter him. He created an art studio with a friend, and as a show of commitment bought five thousand dollars' worth of supplies and became a full-time artist in training.

One morning some time later, Andy awoke and felt something was shifting. He went to his studio, sat before one of his paintings, and began to pray. When he raised his head, he saw a ball of light come through the wall and enter his forehead:

> *The ball enveloped my body, filling me with pure love, pure energy. . . . I found myself communicating with three men. They were definitely my angels. . . . They had beards, whitish hair, very light in color, very bright. . . . They were giving me information telepathically, and told me exactly what I was to do: I was to paint 2,000 paintings by the year 2000. These angels would take care of everything. . . . I knew they would give me my art technique; they would teach me to paint.*

The angels vanished, but kept their word. Soon, through a series of fateful coincidences, Andy Lakey stumbled onto the highly unorthodox technique that marks his paintings — the paint rises off his canvases, so thickly textured it is often applied with tubes.

In little more than a month after this second vision, Andy had completed six canvases. On the day that he put three of these paintings on display at a local bank, a Canadian art collector came in, stared at them for an hour, and ended up hiring Andy to do a giant painting in his home. An art consultant impressed by Andy's unique style — his almost three-dimensional paintings are as tactile as they are visual — suggested that he create paintings for the blind. After the art consultant tipped off a local TV news crew about this talented angel artist, Andy Lakey's career took off.

News anchor Peter Jennings obtained and donated one of Lakey's first paintings to New York City's Lighthouse Inc., a nonprofit organization for the visually impaired. Admirers and owners of his work include Ray Charles, Stevie Wonder, Jimmy Carter, Ronald Reagan, and numerous other high-profile public figures, along with many more people who are deeply moved by his work.

Ten months after Andy began painting, with around fifty paintings under his belt, he had a one-man exhibit in a local gallery. Every single painting sold. He began donating paintings to hospitals, schools for the blind, and other charitable institutions, and now donates 30 percent of his work. Even the pope formally accepted one of Andy's paintings as a gift; it now resides in the Vatican.

Thousands of people have written, faxed, and called Andy Lakey, many reporting different forms of healing, revelation, and transformation in connection with his work. In 1993, Andy, who had by then completed 1,678 angel paintings, went on the *Oprah Winfrey Show* and shared his vision with millions of viewers.

Although some suggest that Andy's vision was no more than

a drug-induced hallucination, his transformed life and the dramatic emergence of his unique artistic gifts suggest otherwise.

Andy, who went on to marry and who has four children, said:

I don't have the answer. I'm just doing what I was instructed to do. Once you love yourself and you love others, it's as if the world knows this, and the world will take care of you and love you back. When I look up at the night sky, I see the stars totally differently . . . they're a reminder of what's really out there. In my heart and spirit I see bright planets and poles of light. I see angels flying through the universe, doing the work of God.

REMEMBER THE MUSIC

A New Life beyond Fear of Death

When Carol Benjamin was nine years old, music entered her life in the sensuous shape of a cello. For twenty-five years, her music graced the practice halls of her home, her schools, the Oberlin College Conservatory, and finally the Fort Wayne Philharmonic Orchestra.

Carol's early life seemed blessed with talent, music, and love. At twenty-three she met and eventually married a kind and gentle man named David. Despite David's struggle with chronic depression, they lived and loved in a world of music, literature, and the outdoors. But in their twelfth year of marriage, David died suddenly, and all semblance of sanity, meaning, and justice left her world. "Part of me wanted to die, too," Carol said. "It was like a temptation from the other side, like standing on a high cliff and looking down."

Within three years of David's death, Carol learned that she had cancer of the liver. Rejecting the option of a transplant, she found a surgeon willing to try to remove the tumor. To prepare for the surgery she began to train daily: She swam, meditated, and watched her diet. Facing her mortality for the first time, she tapped into what she called "warrior energy." With seven-eighths of her liver to be removed, she would have only a fifty-fifty chance — a coin toss — of surviving surgery. So Carol put her things in order, made out a will, left copious instructions, and wrote every friend she had ever known to complete any unfinished business.

At one point, while under general anesthesia, the oddest thing happened: Carol found herself standing at a threshold between worlds, hearing a conversation between two groups of beings — she heard rather than saw them. As if her fate were being discussed in some kind of cosmic courtroom, she heard one group say, in essence, "She's done what she came to do, and she should go now."

"You're right," the other group responded, "but we think she can do more." Carol had a clear sense that either way would be okay; it was out of her hands. Suddenly a hand came from behind and turned her around, away from the threshold, back toward life.

But she hovered on the edge of death for four weeks.

Carol's doctor told her sister, Marla, to prepare herself: It was unlikely that Carol would live. But she did, fighting her way back to a relatively normal life. She moved to Boulder, Colorado, and continued working as a physical therapist, a profession she had learned during her years with David. She even got a puppy.

But Carol was living on borrowed time; her liver grew back to its normal size, yet surgical scars now blocked the bile ducts. With each passing month, her skin yellowed as she grew weaker and more ill. Carol's physician urged her to consider a transplant. Without it, he said, she had only a few more months.

The evaluation process for a liver transplant involved exploratory surgery to determine whether the cancer had spread. If it had, there was no hope; if it hadn't, she would qualify for the lifesaving surgery.

While lying in bed in the pre-op ward, Carol again encountered a being from the other world:

This time, it seemed more like an angelic intervention: Eight of us were scheduled for a variety of operations that morning. The charge nurse announced the surgery order for each of us; I was number six.

I had closed my eyes and was resting, trying to meditate. At one point I opened my eyes and saw a figure standing before me at the foot of my bed — an androgynous being about nine feet tall, wearing a flowing white gown — he appeared to be about nineteen years old, yet ageless. He noticed me looking at him; his expression told me it was okay that I saw him.

I felt an incredible peace. This was my first taste of what I would call grace. Prior to this time, I hadn't the faintest notion of what grace meant, and certainly had no prior experience with angels!

Yet here was this being, visiting the bed of every patient — touching each of them as if giving a blessing. But he wasn't touching them in the order they would be called in for surgery, and I became concerned that someone might be called in before this being could bless them. Just then the nurse came in and told several people their surgery had been delayed for various reasons — it turned out that the angel had touched each person in the exact order they were now scheduled for surgery.

Carol's surgery went well — she was free of cancer — but her liver was in much worse shape than her surgeon had anticipated. He kept her in the hospital for three days, hoping a liver would become available. When none appeared, she finally went home.

Soon she had deteriorated near the point in liver failure where most people just go to sleep, sink into a coma, and never reawaken.

During this twilight time, Carol began spending more time on "the other side." There she met a new group of beings who seemed to be preparing her to cross over. They came to her in the daytime, and at night she went to the other side to be with them in the dream state. She experienced a continuity between the worlds before and after death.

Carol, an extremely down-to-earth person, related all this matter-of-factly:

I felt so cared for by these beings — they felt like friends with whom I had shared a hundred lifetimes. When I saw them it was like I was going home. And I felt a joyous remembrance that they had always been there — but that somehow I'd forgotten this wonderful truth. It was as if I'd had amnesia all these years.

I gave myself up completely to whatever was to be. I told them, "If I'm needed to serve, then I trust you'll keep me alive; if I'm not needed to serve, then I'll go." Then the Saturday night before my transplant, David came to me in my dreams and said in his English accent, "Hang on, luv — just a little longer — it's not your time."

From that moment on, Carol was certain that David's visit had kept her going.

One evening two days later, as she lay on her sofa watching the film *Resurrection*, the phone rang. Too exhausted to rise, Carol heard the voice of the transplant nurse on her answering machine: "I hope you're there and hear this soon, because we have a liver for you." That got her to the phone.

The doctors needed her there in two hours. Carol called a taxi and then her sister Marla, in Ohio, who was at that moment also watching *Resurrection*. Carol headed for the hospital as Marla headed for the airport. In the taxi, Carol gazed through the window at the star-filled sky, knowing it might be her last night.

Carol's transplant, although successful, was marred by complications that triggered a severe illness. At her lowest point, as she lay ill and exhausted, she heard a voice say, "Remember the music." She knew exactly what it meant: Through the dark days, to strengthen her immune system, Carol had visualized herself as a warrior while she played *The Planets*, a stirring symphonic piece by Gustav Holst. At times she had burst into tears, moved by an overwhelming sense of grace.

Now, remembering the music — with the support of her dear David and her otherworldly friends, the sense of grace, and her warrior's energy — Carol made an inner decision to live. "I had had so much help, but now it was my turn, up to me, to my will, to do the fighting. It was like someone had lit a Bunsen burner under me. I was absolutely committed. I felt an energy that was unbelievable."

Carol Benjamin had returned to life.

With her return came a profound commitment to service:

I knew that you don't just get all this help and then do your own thing. It doesn't make sense at any level. I felt an overall sense of being connected to everything, everyone — to life itself. You can't pretend there's a separation between you and other people anymore. It just doesn't work. This experience of grace taught me that extending a helping hand to others, the way it was given to me, is what life is for.

It's great to be alive, but I have no sense of fear of death. It's impossible to fear death, now, because I know those beings are there. But for now, till the time comes to go home, it's a constant call to serve — I can't see my life in any other way. This light has come on. While I live, I'm here to serve. The rest of my life is about finding out what that means.

Carol Benjamin went on to a full and active life of service as a physical therapist (and dog training teacher) in Boulder, Colorado. Although her story is by nature personal and private, she explained in relating it to us, "If it can help bring hope to others, then I'll share it."

LIGHTER THAN AIR

The Extraordinary Feats of a Flying Friar

On the subject of levitation, like that of religion, most of us take one of three positions: believer, nonbeliever, or agnostic. We've all seen people fly, of course — in popular films, on stage, and in our dreams. But few of us, if any, have personally seen a mortal being truly rise up from the earth to float or fly during our normal waking hours. For the empirically minded, it isn't enough to read about it in books; we must see to believe. Yet the fact that we've never seen electricity, or atoms (much less quarks or neutrinos), or Great Aunt Ethel, doesn't seem to faze us.

Faith is selective; we may believe in any number of things, but when it comes to levitation, devotees of gravity may warily cross their arms and smirk. After all, the laws of physics are the laws of physics, aren't they? Well, are we talking Newtonian or quantum? According to the Gospel of Quantum, we are simultaneously energy, light, and matter. And two of those three, as anyone will tell you, are lighter than air.

So the question may be not how another flies, but rather how it is that we do not.

Consider the case of Joseph of Copertino, famed in his own

lifetime as the Flying Friar. Of all reported cases of levitation, the flights of Joseph were likely the most extensively witnessed and documented. Born in 1603, the son of a carpenter, Joseph displayed a religious nature and inclination early in his life. By age eight he experienced and described states of mystical rapture. By sixteen he had entered the Capuchin Order as a monk. For many years Joseph took food only two days a week — on Thursdays and Sundays — and said that he otherwise fed on the "bread of angels."

But even in the monastery, Joseph's otherworldly and impractical nature soon caused him to be sent away. After a brief sojourn he entered another monastery near the town of Copertino, where, at age twenty-five, after years of practicing severe austerities, he became a priest.

Soon after his ordination, Joseph's legendary career as the Flying Friar began, with "a round-trip inaugural flight" in a church in Naples, where he had been sent to defend himself against a charge of heresy before a church tribunal. There, while saying Mass in the presence of a fellow friar and several nuns, Joseph suddenly rose into the air, floated across the church, briefly landed, then rose again and flew back to land at his original point of departure. The charge of heresy against Joseph was dropped; whether this was due to the levitation incident or to other factors was not reported.

On the same journey, soon after this first reported flight, Joseph went to Rome to pay his respects to Pope Urban III. As he knelt to kiss the papal feet, he was again wafted into the air, where he hovered above the astonished pope and his retinue.

Joseph's next stop was a monastery in Assisi; there he levitated fifteen feet in the air, then floated over the heads of dozens of astonished worshippers in order to kiss the feet on the painting of the Virgin Mary placed high on one wall of the chapel.

Without a doubt, such lighthearted reports of a human being flying read like fiction — with more levity than levitation — reminiscent of *Peter Pan and Wendy* or the television series *The Flying Nun*, most likely inspired by Joseph's life.

Yet in the years that followed Joseph's first displays of his divine aerial abilities, hundreds of people, including some of the most respected men and women of their day, personally witnessed and testified to his miraculous and ecstatic flights. Among them were Juan Alfonso Enríquez de Cabrera, Spain's ambassador to Rome; Johan Friedrich, the Duke of Brunswick; the son of Cosimo II of Austria, future cardinal under Pope Clement IX; and of course, Pope Urban III and his exalted retinue.

On more than one occasion, those present who tried to hold Joseph down were lifted into the air with him.

Johan Friedrich, the Duke of Brunswick, was a non-Catholic who traveled to Assisi in 1651 specifically to witness one of Joseph's then-legendary levitations. After witnessing two of Joseph's spontaneous flights, one of which lasted a full fifteen minutes, Friedrich was so overcome with awe that he converted from Lutheranism to Catholicism, which was then tantamount to converting to an enemy faith.

Joseph's most spectacular feat occurred in his monastery garden while he walked with a fellow priest, Friar Antonio Chiarello. Antonio thoughtlessly triggered the episode with a remark to Joseph on the beauty of the heaven God had made. At that point Joseph gave a shriek, went into a rapture, rose into the air, and came to rest kneeling on a fragile branch atop an olive tree, where he remained lost in ecstasy for half an hour. The slender branch, Friar Antonio reported, barely quivered beneath Joseph. When at last the Flying Friar recovered his senses, he could not get down from the tree; Friar Antonio had to fetch a ladder and help him descend.

In 1653, due to his widespread fame and the passion aroused in the public over his numerous miraculous flights and healings, Pope Innocent X ordered that Joseph be transferred to an isolated monastery on Mount Carpegna, and allowed only to come into contact with his brother monks.

The thousand-page Vatican report compiled on Joseph cited more than seventy levitations witnessed by others in Copertino, not counting the frequent levitations that occurred during daily Mass in the presence of his brother monks, nor the numerous levitations, witnessed by others, that occurred in his various travels over the years.

D. Scott Rogo, in his book *Miracles*, wrote:

> The evidence authenticating St. Joseph's levitations is awesome. [They were] publicly observed by both his friends and total strangers; we have numerous firsthand accounts of them; they were not secret events but often occurred in public places; and they do not rest merely on St. Joseph's own word. In short, the testimony pertinent to St. Joseph's levitations is a perfect rebuttal to the types of criticism to which St. Teresa's levitations are prone.

Based on this abundant testimony to Joseph of Copertino's miraculous powers, Pope Benedict XIV declared him blessed in 1753.

SHAMANIC INITIATION

Awakening to Service in Copper Canyon

By the time Mexico's rain-swollen Urique River swept Don Jacobs underwater, into a narrow stone corridor in Copper Canyon in February 1983, his life had reached an impasse.

Born in 1946, Don was raised in a family plagued by alcoholism, which eventually killed his father and imprisoned his mother. Don's way of coping was to be the strong one; he largely raised his two younger sisters and vented his quick temper in athletics. When he grew older, he joined the Marines and became a pilot during the Vietnam War. He often sought his adventure in dangerous pastimes — flying missions, racing wild horses, and riding rapids.

But Don's strength could sometimes be a liability when it took the form of an aggressive, self-righteous temperament — the very temperament that had threatened his marriage, jeopardized his job as a firefighter, complicated his life, and driven him to seek a transforming adventure in the isolated canyon in Central Mexico. Don somehow needed to risk these notorious rapids that ranked among the most treacherous on the continent.

Copper Canyon, in some places four times wider and two

thousand feet deeper than the Grand Canyon, is inhabited by the Raramuri Indians, a tribe renowned for their endurance in running hundred-mile races along the canyon's steep, rocky trails. An endurance runner himself, as well as an avid kayaker, Don had come to the canyon with his friend Dave, hoping to ride the Urique and observe these legendary Indian runners firsthand. His interest in Indians came partly from his own native ancestry; his great grandfather was a full-blooded Cherokee.

A short, stocky Indian named Luis had guided them down into the canyon. Barefoot and carrying a heavy pack, Luis led them on a ten-hour hike along steep trails of jagged rocks, "through a maze of immense chasms" to the Urique River.

The next morning, Don and Dave mounted their inflatable kayaks and started down the river. Their first day was exhilarating. The river coursed along at a manageable twelve hundred cubic feet per second. But on the second afternoon heavy rains began to fall; within an hour the river had swelled to a churning deluge. Don, with Dave following behind, rode the muddy white-water rapids through an obstacle course of massive boulders jutting out of the river, testing their skills to the limit.

Then, unexpectedly, Don entered what appeared to be a quiet pool exiting through a narrow channel just ahead between two immense boulders. Lulled by the deep pool's apparent calm, he realized too late the water's deception, as the full surging might of the rain-swollen river forced him into the bottleneck of a channel too narrow for his raft to pass through. At the mouth of the channel he saw a boiling maelstrom of sticks and leaves being sucked down and swallowed with tons of water.

Paddling furiously in a futile effort to avoid being swallowed as well, Don found himself lodged in the stone chasm, clinging desperately to his raft with one hand while pressing the other against the stone as the water rushed over and beneath him until, finally, his strength gave out.

As Don later reported:

Suddenly, a mysterious calm overcame me. A heightened sense of awareness propelled me into a state of consciousness where fear became a vibratory sensation. I continued searching for a way to survive, but something told me that what was about to happen was important and that I should not fear it.

As these feelings pulsed through me like a current of electricity, a violent wave suddenly flipped my boat. I disappeared into the cold, wet darkness of the hole. When I went under, all my experience informed me that I would certainly drown; even so, a remarkable feeling of calm and peace came over me again. I relaxed completely and surrendered to the river.

In the next few moments, my entire life passed before me in a series of snapshots. With each image, I sent out loving thoughts to the characters and experiences they depicted. I embraced my family and friends. I prayed for Dave's survival and safe return home....

I sensed a radiant white glow of energy swirling about me. Just as I ran out of air and was about to drink the river into my lungs, the tunnel spit me out into the hazy daylight.

Dave, who had seen Don struggling in the chasm and paddled quickly to shore, now made his way downstream. To his amazement and relief, he found Don alive on the bank. The rain poured down in torrents as they climbed into a cave in the rocks, where they remained for three days until the rain stopped.

Don felt an immediate difference in himself, but he wasn't yet aware of the depth of the changes that would occur in him over time. For one thing, he had always enjoyed a good rapport with horses, but in the weeks after his return from Copper Canyon, an unusual ability to communicate with horses awakened in him. He first noticed it with Corazón, his formerly wild mustang — a horse so difficult and unruly that Don had decided to release him in the wild after his return from the canyon. Now Don found he was able to ride Corazón with ease. Where before he had needed reins and muscular force to direct Corazón, Don could now ride him bareback and direct him with mental commands — with nothing more than his thoughts.

"I discovered in myself, apparently from nowhere, an ability to 'talk' to wild horses — so remarkable that it was eventually covered on national television and in almost every equestrian magazine in the country," Don wrote in his book *Primal Awareness*.

By closely observing his unusual new ability, Don discovered that it had something to do with the intense concentration often associated with fear. This "fear effect" appeared to create a heightened state of awareness that made telepathic communication possible. Don would later use this same understanding to communicate with troubled youth — to put them in a state in which they could more quickly make positive shifts in attitude and behavior. Don also began to understand how this same state of fear had led to his life-transforming near-death awakening in the Urique River.

Intrigued, Don continued to observe himself, noting the sometimes subtle changes in his character: "I found myself to be more forgiving and more patient — reflection replaced reaction. . . . I no longer thought of truth as definite and unyielding but rather as something woven into both sides of an issue . . . a new energy and a new direction took hold of me."

Only later was he to learn that the same stone chasm in the

river where he had nearly drowned was an ancient traditional initiation site of the Raramuri shamans. There, aspirants were tossed into the watery vortex of the passage; those who relaxed — who surrendered to the river's power — were, like Don, swept into the channel from which they would be delivered reborn. Those who tensed and struggled found themselves in a bottleneck crack with no escape. Failing the initiation typically meant death by drowning.

Having survived that passage himself, Don now understood at a much deeper level the nature of fear, and its potential as a window to heightened states of awareness in which latent abilities could be awakened and lessons learned. By incorporating the use of spontaneous hypnosis, he began to apply his insights in his work as an emergency medical technician with the fire department.

Don first applied his new understanding to a man named Joe who had been accidentally electrocuted. Shortly after Don and his partner Frank arrived on the scene, Joe went into convulsions and his heart stopped. They put him on the oxygen mask and began CPR. Don, an EMT for years, had participated in numerous life-and-death situations. This time something felt different: "I was no longer merely a technician, grasping at words that seemed appropriate," he said. "I felt empowered to move energy in an invisible world I shared with Joe, and I discerned a connection with a spiritual aspect of him. I knew this part was as important as his physical body."

In the presence of Joe's wife, Don spoke to Joe, then clinically dead, instructing him how to start his heart again. Minutes later, as the paramedics arrived, Joe's heart resumed beating. Later, these paramedics called Don's supervisor and asked "what the deal" was with Don Jacobs telling dead people to start their own hearts again

— Joe's wife had told them that Don had talked her husband back to life.

Don was reprimanded, but that same day Joe himself called from the hospital to thank Don for his instructions and support. Joe, while clinically dead, had apparently heard and could remember everything Don had said to him. He also credited Don's instructions with his return to life.

This was the first in a series of remarkable successes. Using these new methods with his emergency patients, Don found he had new capacities:

> *I was able to speak directly to a deeper part of their psyches, and through my directives, people were taking amazing control of their autonomic nervous systems — coming out of shock, stopping their bleeding, and controlling their blood pressure in response to my suggestions. Later, using the same methodology on myself, I underwent deep abdominal surgery without anesthesia.*

At first, Don's unusual but highly effective methods became standard procedure where he worked. But even though they raised Don's sector's CPR survival rate well above the national average, they proved too controversial within the organization, and their use was eventually forbidden.

Then, in 1997, while surfing the Internet, Don happened upon an article describing the current plight of the Raramuri Indians of Copper Canyon and the indigenous peoples of the surrounding area of the Sierra Madre: Due to the pernicious influence of drug traffickers and illegal loggers, aided by corrupt police and military, native timberlands were being ravaged and the Indians chased off their land or forced by threat of violence to grow marijuana and opium instead of the corn by which they lived. These Indians were also routinely beaten, tortured, and frequently murdered.

Don decided to return to the canyon where his life had been transformed, to see if he could somehow help. On this second trip to Copper Canyon, Don met a hundred-year-old shaman named Agustín Ramos. In Agustín, Don witnessed extrasensory abilities similar to those that had spontaneously awakened in him after his visit fourteen years earlier. By working with Agustín and serving the Raramuri Indians of Copper Canyon, Don reconnected to his own lost Indian heritage.

Don Trent Jacobs, who came to be known as Four Arrows, went on to serve for a time as a professor in the education department of South Dakota's Oglala Lakota College on the Pine Ridge Indian Reservation. In his book *Primal Awareness*, Four Arrows called for public awareness and support of the endangered Raramuri Indians of Copper Canyon. He also encouraged others to explore the shamanic consciousness within their own psyches — the same awareness awakened in him by his brush with death on the Urique River, a gift that continued to illuminate his life.

THE COKEVILLE MIRACLE

A Terrorist Threat and Angelic Intervention

On May 16, 1986, the little town of Cokeville, Wyoming, became the site of a potentially devastating tragedy. At one o'clock that afternoon, white supremacist David Young and his wife, Doris, rolled a shopping cart loaded with powerful gasoline bombs, rifles, and handguns into the Cokeville Elementary School. Young was the town's former marshal, fired for incompetence and reckless behavior.

"This is a revolution and I'm taking your school hostage," he told the startled school secretary. "Don't set off any alarms or make any calls or you and all the children will die." With that, Young and his wife herded 150 children and several teachers — nearly a third of the town's population — into a large classroom.

Young's demand: Within ten days, he and his wife must receive three hundred million dollars from the United States government and a personal phone call from President Ronald Reagan, or they would detonate the incendiary bombs. There would be no negotiations.

Young's diaries later revealed his real plan — get the money, then blow up himself, his wife, and the children. The town of

Cokeville would pay, and Young would have his revenge. A severely disturbed man, he believed they would all reincarnate "in a more evolved dimension." He had more than enough explosives to carry out his threat. Two weeks before, he had gone to an isolated range and set off a test bomb, producing an enormous fireball more than sufficient to incinerate a schoolroom full of children.

For nearly two and a half hours, crowds of anxious parents and friends, as well as news media and other onlookers, waited behind the police lines in a tense vigil, hoping and praying for a safe resolution — even a miracle.

The siege ended two and a half hours after it began, with a cataclysmic explosion. Minutes before that, Young had handed his wife, Doris, the bomb trigger and gone to the bathroom. According to evidence gathered at the scene, Doris detonated the bomb, apparently by accident — only yards away from fifty children huddled in the back of the class.

Immediately after the explosion, Doris Young, now engulfed in flames, staggered out the door and met David in the hall. He shot her once in the head — a mercy killing — and shot and wounded a teacher running down the hall, then returned to the bathroom and shot himself.

According to eyewitnesses in front of the school, bright orange fire engulfed the classroom. The whole town, by then gathered outside, watched in horror as black smoke poured out the windows. As they rushed toward the classroom, now a burned-out shell, the ammunition stockpiled in the bottom of Young's cart went off in the blast, and bullets streaked through the room.

The police chief's daughter, Barbara Frederickson, described the scene as it appeared just after the blast had gutted the room where the children were held hostage. "We heard a big boom and then children came out screaming. The teachers were crawling around on the floor and throwing children out the windows. The entire room was on fire." In the inferno after the blast, thirty-two people received second-degree burns to their faces, and one child was hit by a stray bullet. But none of their injuries was life threatening. Incredibly, all the hostages survived.

But the miracle that had happened in the town of Cokeville, Wyoming, wasn't fully revealed until children separately began to describe to their parents, rescue workers, and police "beings of light" who had come "down through the ceiling." First-grader Nathan Hartley saw them and knew right away they were angels. Rachel and Katie Walker said they were "bright like lightbulbs," and that one hovered over each of the hostages.

The angel hovering over Nathan told him she was his great grandmother, and warned him, "The bomb is going to explode and the two bad people are going to die." She then told him, "Go stand near the window."

Another angel told Katie the same thing. Katie's brother Travis heard a clear voice tell him to take his sisters to the window and keep them there, and that they would be all right. Still another six-year-old child said, "A lady told me that a bomb was going to go off soon; she said go to the window and hurry out."

Other children also saw, heard, or felt the presence of these beings.

"I can't begin to tell you how lucky they were," testified bomb expert Richard Haskell of the Sweetwater County Sheriff's Department. "When you look in that classroom — when you see all that charred furniture and burnt walls — it's amazing that there weren't 150 kids lying in there dead. To call it a miracle would be the understatement of the century."

FROM SWORD TO SPIRIT

A Warrior's Awakening

H is sinewy body wielded the power of death, until he awakened and discovered a new way of living. This is how one of the greatest warriors in history began to teach the invincible power of love.

Morihei Ueshiba was not always a man of peace. Born in Japan in 1883, he fought as an infantryman in the Russo-Japanese war, and later battled pirates and bandit clans in Mongolia. A seasoned soldier and martial arts master, tested in life-and-death battles, Morihei became a martial arts instructor in Japan's elite military academies.

Yet Morihei had a sensitive and religious side, and the human folly he had seen firsthand — violence, greed, corruption, starvation, and war — troubled him. Fate had drawn him into the heart of the world's brutality, but his spirit moved him to seek a solution to this parade of human suffering that passed daily before his eyes.

Morihei Ueshiba became a warrior on a spiritual quest.

A major turning point occurred in the spring of 1925 when, at the age of forty-two, Morihei was attacked by a high-ranking swordsman expertly wielding a razor-sharp sword, or *katana*. Morihei, himself unarmed, defeated his opponent — not by injuring him but by skillfully evading all his cuts, slashes, and thrusts. Elated by this unconventional victory, he walked, in an inspired state, into his garden.

He related the event that followed:

Suddenly the earth trembled. Golden vapor welled up from the ground and engulfed me. I felt transformed into a golden image, and my body seemed as light as a feather. All at once I understood the nature of creation: the Way of a Warrior is to manifest Divine Love, a spirit that embraces and nurtures all things. Tears of gratitude and joy streamed down my cheeks. I saw the entire earth as my home, and the sun, moon, and stars as my intimate friends. All attachment to material things vanished.

Morihei Ueshiba went on to found the flowing martial art of Aikido, translated as "Way of Blending with Spirit," or simply "Art of Peace," whose key principles are harmony and love in action.

Ueshiba later had other visions, insights, and illuminations, and various supernormal abilities were awakened in him. One particular incident reveals not only his uncanny speed but his extraordinary perceptual abilities. Morihei was confronted by a jealous suitor of the woman Morihei was engaged to. The man, a military officer, aimed and fired a single-shot pistol directly toward the center of Morihei's chest at nearly point-blank range, intent on killing his rival. Morihei later reported that at the instant the would-be assassin's finger pulled the trigger, he "felt a pellet of light" strike his chest. At precisely the same instant the bullet exploded from the gun barrel, Morihei turned his body, moving just millimeters out of its path, eluding the bullet. After this, Morihei Ueshiba was regarded as "one who could dodge bullets."

Into his eighties O-Sensei (Great Teacher) Ueshiba could move at impossible speeds and "see" opponents behind his back; he was recorded on film moving a distance of three feet, from inside to outside a circle of attackers, in the space of a single frame of film (or one twenty-fourth of a second); in the film he seems to disappear and reappear. Able to direct his powerful energy through and beyond his body, Ueshiba could effortlessly throw trained martial artists, even those with weapons, and pin them to the mat without touching them, even from several feet away, a feat witnessed by many, and also documented on film.

One of Ueshiba's most powerful and accomplished disciples was Aikido master Koichi Tohei (author of several books on applying ki, or spiritual energy, in daily life). Yet Ueshiba, in his later years a wisp of a man, wielded a power transcending the limits of his slight frame. As one instructor observed, "Trying to push over Tohei is like trying to push over a mountain; but trying to push over O-Sensei was like trying to push over a feather — and not being able to do it." This was the grace of Master Ueshiba, who declared, "The Art of Aikido is invincible, because it contends with nothing."

Morihei Ueshiba, master of the arts of war, evolved into a spiritual sage, a peaceful warrior who lived and taught a way of life based in harmony and devoted to reconciliation. His art of Aikido, whose principles were revealed to him in a moment of illumination, has benefited the lives of many thousands of people worldwide.

"The Way of the Warrior," he wrote, "has been misunderstood ... those who seek competition are making a grave mistake ... the real way of a warrior is the way of peace, the power of love."

FROM HACK WRITER TO POETIC GENIUS

The Mysterious Transformation of Walt Whitman

On Long Island, New York, on May 31, 1819, a child was born who would grow from an ordinary seedling into literary giant. Yet for the first half of his life, Walt's greatness, and even his potential for it, were nowhere in evidence. And this is the mystery at the heart of our story.

Walt, an adventurous boy, was raised in a farmhouse built by his father's hand, on a farm populated by chickens, pigs, and apple orchards, with herds of sheep and cattle nearby. Walt survived the cholera epidemic of the early 1830s that killed millions. At age twelve, by chance, he entered the trade of journalism, working as a typesetter's apprentice at a local newspaper.

In time, Walt's experience in the newspaper trade, as well as his physical·size and strength, gave him a natural authority and self-confidence — and an explosive temper. From age twenty to thirty Walt worked as a journalist, printer, and editor in the rough-and-tumble early-American newspaper trade. In an era when editors of competing papers fought verbal brawls in print, Walt flung himself into the fray, making friends and enemies aplenty. He slandered, maligned, and baited his enemies, and trumpeted his opinions from the public soapbox of his editorial columns. According to Justin Kaplan in *Walt Whitman: A Life*, the young journalist "could be seen kicking a politician downstairs, man-handling a church attendant, and grappling with a carpetbag senator who had insulted him."

Although journalism had much to recommend it, Walt aspired to success at poetry and fiction. But the fruits of his first fifteen years of creative writing were a mediocre and deservedly forgotten body of work consisting largely of bombastic, third-rate poetry, syrupy short stories, clumsy romantic morality tales, and hack adventure novels — the overripe harvest of a profoundly unoriginal, uninspired mind. Biographer Kaplan described them as "full of shabby melodrama, false sentiment, and gothic dodges . . . derivative and imitative, preachy and didactic, dripping with false sentiment, cliché, and melodramatic contrivance."

Kaplan's appraisal of Whitman's work to that time garners universal agreement among scholars.

No one could have predicted the genius and originality that would burst forth out of nowhere, suddenly in full bloom at the age of thirty-five, in Whitman's epic *Leaves of Grass*, after an almost five-year literary silence.

Although Whitman's poetry, both earthy and transcendent, spoke of his illuminations and furnished abundant clues that point to otherworldly inspiration, Walt never directly explained what happened to him during that five-year period. We only know that an entirely new energy flooded into his work — a poetic voice rendering profound insights into life, death, sex, humanity, love, the body, and eternity, from the intimate perspective of an earthy mystic.

Richard Bucke, Whitman's personal physician and disciple,

and author of *Cosmic Consciousness*, commented on Whitman's mysterious transformation from mediocre hack to illumined genius: "The line of demarcation between the two Whitmans is perfectly drawn . . . writings of absolutely no value were immediately followed by pages across each of which, in letters of ethereal fire, are written . . . such vital sentences as have not been written ten times in the history of the race."

Whitman's poetry now expressed eternal truths with a stunning vitality, originality, and power rarely achieved by Western writers before him, except perhaps Shakespeare — a revelation of the spirit alive in all of earthly life, in everything and everyone.

Unlike many mystics, Walt's visions did not separate him from the world; instead, he awakened into the world: into his body and his earthly desires, and into his full humanity. In the following poem, Whitman describes a moment of fleshy grace, lifting him from mediocrity to genius and catapulting him into life with an impassioned sensuality and sublime eroticism that, while shocking to the Victorian era, was to him nothing less than sacred:

> *I believe in you my soul . . .*
> *I mind how once we lay such a transparent summer morning,*
> *How you settled your head athwart my hips and gently turned*
> *over upon me,*
> *And parted the shirt from my bosom-bone, and plunged your*
> *tongue to my bare-stripped heart,*
> *And reached till you felt my beard, and reached till you held*
> *my feet.*
> *Swiftly arose and spread around me the peace and knowledge*
> *that pass all the argument of the earth,*
> *And I know that the hand of God is the promise of my own,*
> *And I know that the spirit of God is the brother of my own,*

> *And that all the men ever born are also my brothers, and the*
> *women my sisters and lovers,*
> *And that a kelson of the creation is love. . . .*

Singing ecstatic hymns in a tone and tempo unfamiliar to his time, in a voice universal yet uniquely American, Whitman leaped in a single bound into the rarefied company of literary immortals. His mysterious illumination transformed not only his work, but also his identity and character — a change visible even in his photographs. In his fifties, during the Civil War, Walt volunteered as a nurse in the camps along the battlefields, and devoted himself for the duration of that hellish war to relieving the suffering of combatants on both sides of the conflict. His biographer estimated that Walt made over six hundred hospital visits, and in one form or another had ministered to nearly a hundred thousand sick and wounded soldiers.

Walt was deeply loved by the young, often tragically wounded soldiers whose lives he touched and changed. Most of them remembered him the rest of their lives, and many corresponded with him for years after the war ended.

We can only speculate concerning the precise nature and time of the extraordinary events that led to Whitman's transformation, but his words testify to its reality, for even in the terrible carnage of the war, he could say, "I see something of God in each hour of the twenty-four, and in each moment then. In the faces of men and women I see God, and in my own face in the glass. I find letters from God dropped in the street, and every one is signed by God's name."

Whitman's transformed character and presence turned people toward him like flowers to sunlight. In his old age he was surrounded by many who regarded him as a beloved teacher. In describing this literary genius, Richard Bucke wrote:

[H]is outward life, his inward spiritual existence and his poetry were all one . . . indeed, no man who ever lived liked so many things and disliked so few. . . . For young and old his touch had a charm that cannot be described. This charm, if understood would explain the whole mystery of the man, and how he produced such effects not only upon the well, but among the sick and wounded.

Bucke went on to describe Whitman's brief meeting with one of those who sought his company:

Whitman only spoke to him about a hundred words altogether, and these quite ordinary and commonplace; but shortly after leaving [Whitman] a state of mental exaltation set in that lasted six weeks. . . . I may add that this person's whole life has been changed by that contact . . . in an extraordinary degree.

Even now, on the edge of a slow-moving stream somewhere or in a grassy mountain meadow, lovers may be reading aloud the words of Walt Whitman, America's saintly blue-collared rogue, whose inspired gospel of earthy divine love still sounds "over the rooftops of the world."

HIDDEN BLESSINGS

When Bad Luck Becomes Good Fortune

Born in the late 1940s in Southern California, Danny Millman was raised in blissful ignorance in a middle-class home of hardworking parents, with an older sister, a dog, and two cats. He grew up in the seeming fantasy world of the 1950s — a world of schoolyards, friends, games, sports, and double-feature movies on weekends. He did all the things he was supposed to do — working hard, being good, and living up to his parents' expectations.

Small and wiry, Danny inherited his mom's smarts and his dad's strength. He loved climbing trees, swinging like Tarzan, and jumping off the garage roof with a parachute made of an old sheet. Then his junior high school homeroom teacher started a trampoline and tumbling club. That year Danny came alive in a new way: He had found his passion.

By the age of fourteen he had won a state trampoline championship; while still in high school he won the U.S. Championships and performed in Europe. Then, in his freshman year at U.C. Berkeley, he won the first World Trampoline Championships in London. That's when Danny began training toward a spot on the U.S. Olympic Gymnastics Team.

Life had taught Danny that he could control his own destiny, as long as he did the right thing and worked hard. Now life had other lessons to teach.

Near summer's end, before a senior year filled with promises of glory, Danny packed for an upcoming trip to then-Yugoslavia, where he was being sent by the U.S. Gymnastics Federation as an elite gymnast and potential Olympian, to train with the best gymnasts on earth at the World Championships — a final stepping-stone to the Olympic Trials and Games beyond. It seemed as if his whole life had directed him toward this goal.

On his last evening in Los Angeles before catching his flight, Danny visited his sister. Then, an hour later, as he headed home on his Triumph motorcycle, his life was abruptly transformed by an event that seemed far less than divine. There were no visions, no blissful revelations, no angelic voices — only the thud of metal against metal, the sound of shattering glass, and a terrible crunch of bones. And then, unbelievable pain.

In his book *Way of the Peaceful Warrior*, author Dan Millman tells what happened: "I had no clue that my life was about to change as I drove carefully, observing the speed limit, wearing a helmet. I was about to learn that being good and doing the right thing may sometimes make no difference at all."

The older-model white Cadillac facing him in the intersection, waiting to make a left turn, knew nothing of his future plans. As Danny entered the intersection, the driver, who didn't see him, gunned his accelerator and turned directly in front of him.

Danny had a half second to choose what he would do: Swerve right and hit the car head-on? Swerve left into oncoming traffic he couldn't see? Lay the bike down, slide, and perhaps be crushed beneath the car's wheels? Instead, he made a decision he was to replay over and over in the coming days: He jammed on his brakes, hoping to slow down enough to avoid serious injury on impact.

It wasn't enough.

Danny slammed into the right bumper, shattering his femur, his right upper leg bone, in nearly forty pieces. According to one eyewitness, his body did a one and one-half somersault over the top of the Cadillac before crashing to the concrete on his back. When Danny regained consciousness, he looked up to see a circle of faces looking down at him. He heard an ambulance, then saw something white sticking out of his torn sneaker: All the toes of his left foot were dislocated and fractured. In shock, he asked the ambulance driver, "Is that white thing sticking through my shoe one of my bones?"

"Yeah," said the ambulance driver, unsympathetic to motorcycle riders. Then, taking a look at Danny's right leg, he added, "But that's the least of your worries." Danny became aware of a searing pain. The rest was a blur of constant, throbbing agony — the emergency room, a tired doctor who hand-drilled a bolt through Danny's right knee with only a shot of local anesthetic, his ashen-faced parents. Still in shock, Danny asked the doctor if his leg would be healed soon because he had to be ready to train in Yugoslavia in a few days. The doctor didn't even answer.

All the while, a part of him was thinking, "This can't be happening."

The next morning Danny awoke in traction in his hospital room, with the realization dawning that he was not going to the World Championships, not enrolling for classes this semester, not likely going to the Olympics — and maybe never walking normally again. His gymnastics career, the passion of his life and a foundation of his identity, had apparently come to an end.

No one, least of all Dan Millman, would ever have predicted that a turning point would enter his life in the shape of a white Cadillac — or that shattered bones and broken dreams would open doors to a new future that conventional Danny had never even glimpsed.

Three weeks later, after major surgery and a bone transplant — after treading water in a sea of pain in between morphine shots — a quieter, more reflective and compassionate young man, now twenty pounds lighter, left the hospital. His boyhood name, Danny, no longer seemed to fit. So it was Dan who crutched slowly toward the car of a waiting friend who had invited Dan to stay with his family near the beach in Santa Monica, so he could begin a long process of physical rehabilitation.

Dan Millman had entered the hospital a voracious meat eater; he left the hospital a vegetarian. He had always been a cocky, fast-talking kid; now he observed more, and listened thoughtfully. When he finally returned to college, he began intensive rehabilitation and training. As he relearned to walk — first on crutches, then with a cane, and finally with a terrible limp — Dan remained in that reflective space. Inch by painful inch, as he fought his way back — through physical setbacks, self-doubt, and dark depressions, Dan saw clearly how he had been racing down a single path his whole life, with concentration but also with tunnel vision, never looking up to question where he was going or what life was about.

Now he began to ask some of life's larger questions — Who am I? What is life for? — questions that hadn't occurred to him before, at least not with the same impact. Dan began to wonder about death, which had brushed against him that night months before when he had felt nearly invincible. He also wondered about

God, and spirituality both Eastern and Western — not new questions in the world but new for Dan.

As Dan has described it:

It was during this painful period of soul-searching that I stumbled upon an old man late one night, in a Texaco station on the corner of campus — an old man I called "Socrates." I sometimes wonder — would I have met him, or awakened to my current life as a writer and teacher, if I hadn't broken my leg? All I can know is that it served as a catalyst and carried me to this present moment — to my wife, my children, and my calling.

Remarkably, little more than a year later, Dan helped lead his team to win the 1968 NCAA Gymnastics Championships, and was chosen Senior Athlete of the Year. As the years passed, he was appointed head gymnastics coach at Stanford University, later joined the faculty at Oberlin College, and was eventually named to the Berkeley Athletic Hall of Fame and the U.S. Gymnastics Hall of Fame.

But long before, Dan had come to see all such accomplishments as preparation for another path — that of teaching, writing, and service.

The pain of his accident, and the ordeal of recovery, somehow purified and opened Dan to another dimension of reality hidden behind the familiar world he had known:

Sometimes you fall into a dark hole and have a difficult struggle climbing out of it. Then, when you finally get up out of that hole, you appear to be in the same place you were before you fell in. But you're not in the same place, because you're no longer the same person; you've changed in the process. You're stronger, wiser, and more compassionate — you've learned something about yourself and about life....

That accident gave me new perspective I might not have seen any other way. It revealed a bigger picture and divine reality behind the scenes of my life. I've had other spiritual experiences — joyous revelations and mystical openings — in my life, but that "accident" turned out to be one of the best things that ever happened to me. I sure don't recommend breaking bones as a method of spiritual awakening. But when adversity visits — and with it pain, grief, disappointment, or loss — it's good to also notice the hidden gifts and surprising grace that it may also bring, depending on how we respond, and whether we're paying attention.

I recently came across words that spoke directly to my accident and its evolutionary aftermath: Former Senator (and disabled vet) Max Cleland wrote, "I had not always believed that strength could come from brokenness, or that the thread of a divine purpose could be seen in tragedy. But I do now."

As one dream dies, another is born: Dan Millman began writing during his recovery and in the years that followed. Now a bestselling author published in thirty languages, the former athlete has taught people around the world how to live with a peaceful heart and a warrior spirit, sharing lessons he learned in the school of adversity and the classroom of daily life.

GIVING UP TO GOD

The Healing Mission of an Alcoholic

With the possible exception of Jack Daniels, no man's name is more closely associated with alcohol than that of Bill Wilson. His story began, ironically, in a room behind a bar where he was born on November 26, 1895, in East Orson, Vermont.

Bill adored his father, the manager of a marble quarry who played ball with Bill after work. But one day when Bill was ten, his mother took him and his sister out for a picnic and informed them that their father had left for good. Bill never even got to say good-bye.

He wouldn't see his father again for nine years. Although devastated, Bill never spoke of the incident. To manage his turbulent emotions, he vigorously applied himself to sports and music, excelling in both. In the process he cultivated a highly competitive nature.

At sixteen, Bill fell deeply in love with Bertha, a local minister's daughter. This was the happiest year of his life — until the eve of his seventeenth birthday, when the school principal announced to the assembled students that Bertha had died unexpectedly during a minor operation. Bill fell into a deep depression.

Formerly a top student, he now failed his classes and was unable to graduate.

Two years later he met a young woman named Lois, who would, in her way, help shape Bill's destiny. She believed in him, and helped him to once again believe in himself. As his depression lifted, he began to recover the drive he had lost with his first love's death.

By 1915 Bill was back on his feet. After attending college, he joined a military program in Virginia, and at twenty-one he was commissioned as a second lieutenant. Now an officer, Bill was sent to Fort Rodman in Massachusetts, where he attended dinner parties in the homes of the good people of the town. At one of these gatherings, Bill took his first drink.

Socially awkward and self-conscious, Bill soon discovered that alcohol transformed his character: It seemed to put him at ease, loosen his tongue, imbue him with energy and charm, and make him feel connected to others. This seemingly magical potion made Bill the life of every party. But he drank to excess, often passing out by the end of the night.

In 1918 Bill married his sweetheart Lois before shipping off to England to fight in World War I. But by the time he got to France, the war was winding down. Having never made it to the front, Bill returned home determined to succeed at something. He studied law for the next three years, but his drinking continued. Foolishly, he showed up for his bar exam drunk, and failed. Landing on his feet, Bill began dabbling in Wall Street, and by luck or intuition his investments brought him considerable profits. Finding himself a well-to-do young man, he seriously studied the market, and the profits kept rolling in. Bill had found his niche: In 1926 a prestigious Wall Street investment firm hired him at a handsome salary, with an expense account and a thousand-dollar credit for buying stocks. His drinking increased with his fortunes, shaking the foundation of his marriage. At the height of the Roaring Twenties, alcohol seemed a symbol of liberation, and Bill appeared to many to be celebrating his success. Only he and Lois knew he had a problem.

Bill was a successful drunk — his money and charm made his liability seem only a quirk. While he was on top of the world, his company viewed him as a wonder boy, worth his weight in gold. To his friends he was a live wire, a good-time Charlie.

But by 1927 Bill and Lois both realized he was in a fight for his life. He wrote vows of abstinence in the family Bible, but never kept them for long. Bill was living out the pattern of an alcoholic — vows of abstinence followed by drunken binges and bouts of crushing remorse. As countless lost battles with the bottle destroyed his confidence, Bill's desperation deepened, and his employers and associates began raising eyebrows.

Then the stock market crashed in 1929. Now financially ruined, Bill Wilson appeared as he really was — a desperate man in the grip of a terrible malady. Bill, who had once fancied himself a future J. P. Morgan destined to rule a financial empire, was now sixty thousand dollars in debt — a pauper who could not stop drinking to save his life.

Bill now entered the scary phase of alcoholism, terrifying friends and strangers with his insane behavior: He flew into drunken rages, hurled a sewing machine across a room at Lois, roared through his house kicking out door panels, and with his utterly predictable binges, sabotaged his few potential business comebacks.

During Bill's bouts of drunken insanity, Lois feared him. But in his sober moments, when she saw him overwhelmed by remorse and grief at what he had become, she pitied and loved him. She knew that deep inside Bill was a good person — an honest and hardworking man who cared about people. Neither of them understood his problem; alcoholism had not yet been identified as a medical condition.

By late 1933, they had both lost hope. The self-destructive ordeal that Bill's life had become seemed fated to end in his early death. By 1934 he was suicidal, and his binges left him mentally deranged for days. When doctors diagnosed early signs of brain damage, the prospect of madness terrified him into several months of sobriety. For a time his willpower seemed resurrected.

His fall came on Armistice Day, triggered by a celebratory drink "on the house" offered by a patriotic bartender. Lois found him passed out in the street at five in the morning, bleeding from a wound to his head.

He spent the following months on a nonstop binge aimed at the grave, settling into his last bout as into a comfortable, well-worn armchair, holed up in his room. That is where Ebbie T. found him. Ebbie, an old school friend and drinking buddy, had kicked the bottle.

When Bill asked him why he was not drinking, Ebbie replied, "I've gotten religion." Bill would not ordinarily have given this statement much weight; he saw religion as a mere social convention. But Ebbie's sobriety impressed him; Bill knew that Ebbie's drinking problem had been on a par with his own. Ebbie told Bill of a group of down-and-out men, some of them drunks, uniting with one another to overcome their problems — with the help of a higher power, a higher will.

The group's founder, a minister named Rowling, was a former drunk who had been personally treated by the great psychiatrist

Carl Jung. When Rowling relapsed, Jung had told him the only thing that could save him was "a spiritual awakening." Rowling protested that he already believed in God. But Jung said only direct experience could transform him, and he advised Rowling to find a spiritual group that could support this quest.

Jung's advice proved prophetic. Rowling was cured after a mystical experience. Afterward, he founded the Oxford Group, based in teachings of purity, prayers, and surrender. There, Ebbie T. was released from his own slavery to the bottle, given peace of mind, and found happiness such as he had never known. Ebbie's words made Bill want to be sober again, and his example provided a ray of hope. Now all Bill needed to do was pray and surrender his life to a higher power.

There was only one problem: Bill didn't believe in God. He continued drinking while contemplating his inevitable death, until one day, alone in his room, he cried out in desperation, with no faith at all: "If there be a God, let Him show Himself!" He later recalled what happened next:

Suddenly, my room blazed with an indescribably white light. I was seized with an ecstasy beyond description. Every joy I had known was pale by comparison. . . . I was conscious of nothing else for a time. Then . . . there was a mountain. I stood upon its summit where a great wind blew. A wind not of air, but of spirit. In great, clean strength, it blew right through me. Then came the blazing thought, "You are a free man." I became acutely conscious of a Presence, a veritable sea of living spirit. I lay on the shores of a new world; I seemed possessed by the absolute, and the curious conviction that no matter how wrong things seemed to be, there could be no question of the ultimate rightness of God's universe. . . . For the first time, I felt that I really belonged. I knew that I was loved and could love in return.

Bill Wilson would never touch alcohol again. When Lois came home and saw him, she reported, "I knew something overwhelming had happened. His eyes were filled with light. His whole being expressed hope and joy. From that moment on I shared his confidence in the future."

Bill's illumination left him with a deep gratitude for the life given him and an urge to help others — to share the grace he had been given. He began to formulate the idea of a movement of alcoholics who would help one another, a movement that would spread out to "reach every alcoholic in the world capable of being honest enough to admit his own defeat."

Bill Wilson had found his life purpose.

He soon realized that alcoholics couldn't tolerate preaching. He needed an approach uniquely suited to the alcoholic temperament — one that would penetrate their denial, awaken self-understanding, and make them available to grace. The Twelve Steps began evolving in Bill's mind.

Then, a fateful meeting with another alcoholic, Dr. Robert Smith, known as Dr. Bob, catalyzed the birth of Alcoholics Anonymous. Their lasting spiritual partnership would contribute to saving millions of alcoholics from addiction and death, as did the book *Alcoholics Anonymous*.

A first edition of three hundred thousand copies was published in 1939 — and over the decades the book has been read by tens of millions. Today, Alcoholics Anonymous groups meet each day in cities and towns all around the world. Bill Wilson's Twelve Step program — conceived after his awakening and based on principles of self-understanding, service to others, and surrender to a higher power of one's own understanding — has liberated millions of people from the bondage of their addictions and restored them to meaningful and productive lives.

In 1971, on his fifty-third anniversary of marriage to Lois, after years of love and service, Bill Wilson passed away, leaving behind a loving wife and a legacy that will live forever.

REBIRTH OF A MADWOMAN

The Resurrection of Byron Katie

The sudden transformation of Byron Katie serves as a remark-able testimony to the powers of spiritual resurrection that live in each of us.

Born Byron Kathleen Reid in Breckenridge, Texas, in 1942, she was raised in the small desert town of Needles, California, in the years following World War II. Her mother said that she was named Byron for money, after a wealthy relative offered financial support if the child was given his name, and Kathleen for love. Growing up, everyone called her Katie. Her homemaker mother and her father, a railroad worker, saw Katie grow from a quiet, thoughtful little girl into an aggressive, competitive teenager who sought to be the best in everything she did. A top student, she played piano and sang in a regional choir. Beautiful, energetic, and fun, Katie was voted first runner-up for queen of her high school prom.

At nineteen she married Robert, her high school sweetheart. They moved to Fresno; two sons and a daughter soon followed. Robert and Katie formed their own company as equal partners. When her marriage, like many, met with difficulties, Katie, a perfectionist and high achiever, suffered the belief that she was not enough. She began striving for the usual symbols of happiness and security — money, beauty, talent, and success.

Katie invested their mutual earnings in real estate. Within a few years, she and Robert owned shares of numerous buildings in Needles's business district. They bought a grand riverfront house and threw lavish parties attended by an elite and influential local crowd. By the 1970s, Katie had become a millionaire.

Katie now had her long-sought success. She was doing big business, raising a family, living high. But it wasn't enough; nothing pleased or satisfied her. In her increasingly frustrated and ultimately futile search for happiness through money and power, Katie had "bullied, intimidated, and badgered" anyone, even her husband and children, to get her way. But in the midst of having everything and seeking more, her passion had turned to desperation. Her marriage with Robert became a battle of wills, her family life a series of skirmishes. They were all casualties, especially the children. "If I didn't get my way," Byron Katie said, "I would leave the house and take the children with me."

The third time she did this, Robert got involved with another woman.

This was a time of darkness for Katie and for her children, but the seeds had been sown long before. For years she had held back the darkness and emptiness with food, alcohol, tobacco, and constant striving. But her strategy took its toll; her progressive disintegration led to rages, alcohol abuse, and paranoia. At one point she bought a gun and kept it loaded under her bed. Finally, even her children feared her. When her marriage ended in 1976, Katie and the children wound up penniless in Barstow, California.

Then, in 1979, she married Paul, an old friend fifteen years her senior. When Paul was nineteen and Katie four, he had paved the street where she lived. She still recalled being captivated by his laughter; she had loved him even then. Katie and Paul began buying, fixing up, and reselling old houses and were soon quite wealthy — Katie still had the knack. Once again she had money, friends, a thriving career, and a family she loved. But the meaning had drained out of her existence. She felt herself dying inside.

Paul, a good man, had married Katie on her way down. He'd seen a couple of friends have nervous breakdowns. But he'd never witnessed anything like his wife's terrifying descent.

Katie had once taken on the world, charmed people, closed deals, made money. Now, afraid to leave the house, she went weeks without bathing, changing her clothes, or brushing her teeth. She spent days in bed — drinking, smoking, raging, popping codeine, eating ice cream by the gallon. Her weight shot up to over two hundred pounds. Her torment and her rage were unrelieved: "Nothing felt good, nothing made me happy, nothing brought me peace. In the end I was obese and starving. . . . I was in so much pain and the pills weren't working. I was insane, a dead woman still breathing."

Her children spun off in their own mad directions, fleeing their cyclone mother raging on her bed. Paul became Katie's primary caretaker — her buffer to a world she now feared. During the first seven years of their marriage, Paul suffered four heart attacks; the strain of caring for his wife came close to killing him. Katie spent the last two of those years lying on the bed, her unchanged clothing often plastered to her body and her unwashed hair matted to her head.

In 1986, after his fourth heart attack, Paul took Katie, now forty-three, to a halfway house. She lived in the attic, sleeping on the floor. All she wanted was to die.

Then one morning Byron Katie woke up reborn.

The bare facts of this event cannot begin to convey its impact or explain its occurrence. Morning dawned, and Katie stirred, lying on the floor. She opened her eyes and saw a cockroach crawling across a human foot. She did not, in that moment, know what a foot, or for that matter what anything, was. All was a mystery.

Yet the sight of the insect, the foot, the leg, and the room filled her with delight and awe. She was a newborn, gazing in wonder at life. "It was the most amazing thing," she recalled. "I looked at the foot and the leg and I had never seen anything so beautiful and marvelous. It was the same with the floor, with the cockroach, and with the light, seeing it for the first time . . . and the unfolding of it was so incredible . . . total, total joy."

The world was new. Katie had awakened from "an ancient dream." Whatever had previously obscured her view of life's inherent perfection was gone. Now, from moment to moment, she saw and joyously embraced reality exactly as it was. Everything she gazed upon, within and without, glowed with radiant life.

We may never know what catalyzed this simple yet absolute turnaround in perception and consciousness. But one thing was certain: Overnight, Katie had moved from suicidal despair to ecstatic freedom. The madwoman had vanished. In her place appeared a beautiful changeling, an innocent child.

No one, least of all Katie, understood what had happened. Her daughter Roxann at first believed that her mother was playing a trick. Yet she saw a different person come home. "Her face was changed completely," Roxann reported. "Her eyes were cleared. She was not the same person."

Understandably, Roxann feared the return of the madwoman she had known. But what had happened to Katie persisted and only deepened over time. Her past behind her, her future yet to unfold, she now lived in the eternal present. Her contact with everyday reality — with people, objects, and situations — though at times bewildering, continued to fill her with joy.

For a time, Roxann led her mother, still absorbed in a childlike state of awe, around by the hand. Katie would spontaneously hug people on the street — friends, strangers, the homeless — with equal delight. Surprisingly, many let her, perhaps sensing her unconditional love and acceptance.

For seven years after the awakening, inner revelations came to Katie, and she tried to put them into words to share with others: "... there is only love ... there is no time ... unlearning is everything...." But she had leaped across a chasm of consciousness, and no words seemed capable of building a bridge for those who couldn't see to the other side. She said of that time: "I was wild with love, mad with love." But words couldn't convey it. She had to live her realization to sustain it.

Katie stopped trying to tell people what they hadn't asked to hear and began to simply love — to love those she had known, those she had harmed, and those she now met — no longer expecting them to understand, to be good, to love her back, or to be anything other than who they were. Living the truth had nothing to do with changing other people. Who they were, and what they did, was their business. Her only business was to love them unconditionally. By living in this way, Katie gradually regained the trust of the family she had nearly destroyed, and helped to heal them.

One night six months after her awakening, Katie experienced a kind of spiritual agony from the tension of trying to live and love in a world that did not yet understand or accept who she was. An old woman appeared to her, sitting in a chair beside the bed, "a wonderful, voluptuous old lady with her hair tied in a bun." Katie merged into this lady, and found herself looking out through ancient eyes. In this altered state, she saw herself and Paul, lying on the bed, as two primal beings who didn't yet realize that they didn't have to suffer. Life itself was unfolding perfectly.

For the next seven years, the marvelous old woman appeared to guide Katie:

> *What I've come to know is that I projected the lady... like a movie... as a result of painful limitations I was experiencing in this dimension. We give ourselves exactly what we need. We supply our own medicine.... Today I don't wait for angels. I am always the angel I have been awaiting, and so are you. It's not out there, it's in here.... Some people would project Christ, others Krishna.... I projected a fat lady with a bun on her head wearing a paisley dress — that's who I could trust. Now I trust All. I woke up knowing that God is every-thing.... There is no exception in my experience.*

Katie's thoughts returned, of course, as thoughts do — and with them judgments, fears, and expectations. At such times she felt herself slipping from the freedom of her awakening into the mind of suffering. But whenever this happened, she worked her way back by a compassionate vigilance, inspecting the thoughts, beliefs, and false assumptions that separated her from others and set her against life. Doing this "Work," as she called it, returned her gracefully to the pristine awareness of her original awakening.

The Work became her constant practice.

Through this process, and her unconditional acceptance of life, Katie made peace with each moment — and with every event past or present. "All that I went through — every breath," she said, "was what it took for me to finally wake up. All teaches love in the long run. All needs are supplied. . . . Every experience of life is for this."

Byron Katie went on to travel worldwide teaching the Work — the fruit of her past struggles, her extraordinary awakening, and her continual surrender to life as it arises, moment to moment.

TRANSFORMATION AT LOURDES

Healing a Physician's Soul

Born in France in the late 1800s, Alexis Carrel, like many of his contemporaries, received a religious upbringing. But after years of medical school, where he learned to apply rigorous critical analysis to every question, Alexis found his childhood faith implausible; he had acquired the skepticism of a confirmed rationalist.

As a physician, Alexis rejected beliefs in miracles. And when he began to hear stories of "miraculous healings" of numerous afflictions — healings attributed to the waters of Lourdes, he decided that such phenomena must be psychosomatic in origin. No true organic disease such as cancer or tuberculosis could be cured by faith alone — of this he was certain. Yet as a scientist, he was honest enough to realize that disbelief without investigation was little more than negative faith, another side of the same irrational coin.

Because Alexis valued, above all else, the power of reason, he traveled to Lourdes in 1903 in order to investigate these phenomena directly, examining patients before and after they went to the "holy grotto." His first afternoon there he met A. B., a young medic and past classmate volunteering as a stretcher bearer, carrying "cripples" to the waters of the grotto. As he and Alexis discussed cases they had each seen, A. B. mentioned a nun who had been cured that very afternoon of an old ankle injury. But Alexis, who had examined her and found that her injury was not organic, attributed her cure to "auto-suggestion."

Then A. B. sadly mentioned a boy with terminal cancer. The boy had left that morning, uncured, with his brokenhearted father. "You see," said Alexis, "Lourdes is powerless against organic disease."

A. B. quickly responded, "I have seen cases just as serious cured." He then described a string of such cases. Alexis held to his position; as a scientist, he refused to accept as fact anything he had not seen with his own eyes and thoroughly investigated before and after.

"What kind of a disease would you have to see cured to convince you?" A. B. asked.

After considering the patients under his care, Alexis said, "There is one patient who seems closer to death at this moment than any of the others. Her name is Marie Ferrand, an unfortunate girl in the final stages of tuberculosis. I know her history — her whole family died of the same disease. She has tubercular sores, lesions of the lungs, and now has a peritonitis diagnosed both by a general practitioner and by the well-known Bordeaux surgeon, Bromilloux. Her condition is very grave.... She may die any moment. If such a case were cured, it would indeed be a miracle."

Marie Ferrand would be their test case. They immediately went to her bedside in the hospital of Our Lady of the Seven Sorrows, to find that her condition had deteriorated. "Her pulse was excessively rapid, a hundred and fifty beats a minute, and irregular," wrote Alexis. "Her heart was giving out. Her abdomen was also distended, with solid masses and fluids filling her belly, her legs swollen, her nose and hands cold, and her nails and ears had turned a greenish hue. Advanced tubercular peritonitis," Alexis told A. B. "The fluid is almost all gone. You can feel the solid masses at the sides — death is near."

Another doctor examined her, and agreed. "She might very well die at the grotto," he told Alexis softly. Alexis considered his ethical vows; if she was to die in any case, he would do his patient no harm by this investigation. And it might serve the higher good of science. He went ahead to the pool and was waiting there when Marie arrived on a stretcher with A. B.

In his book *Man: The Unknown* — based on detailed notes he took as the events occurred — Alexis described what happened next:

> *The ministering priest was kneeling down, facing the line of patients and the crowds beyond. He lifted his arms and held them out like a cross. He was young; his fleshy white face, dripping with sweat, was covered with red blotches. Only the child-like expression in his eyes and the evident intensity of his faith saved him from absurdity. "Holy Virgin, heal our sick!" he cried out, his child's mouth twisted with emotion . . . the crowd responded with a cry. . . . Here and there, people held out their arms. The sick half-raised themselves on their stretchers. The atmosphere was tense with expectancy. . . . A forest of arms was raised. A wind seemed to blow through the crowd; intangible, silent, powerful, irresistible, it swept over the people.*

Alexis also reported that he felt a catch in his throat and a tremor through his spine. And to his surprise, he suddenly wanted to cry.

After examining other patients in the line, Alexis returned to find Marie Ferrand still hovering at the point of death. Fearing to immerse her in the grotto, lest it hasten her demise, the doctor and the stretcher bearer instead poured water from the grotto over her head. Alexis now looked closely at Marie and noticed that "the harsh shadows on her face had disappeared . . . her skin was somehow less ashen." He assumed his perception of her improvement to be a psychologically induced hallucination, based on hope and suggestion — interesting in itself. He recorded the observation in his notebook, along with the time: twenty minutes before three.

Alexis continued to observe his patient intently, with all the objectivity he could bring to bear, and noted that "there was a distinct improvement of her general appearance. The face of Marie Ferrand slowly continued to change. Her eyes, so dim before, were now wide with ecstasy as she turned them toward the grotto. This change in her visage was undeniable." As yet, this proved nothing.

Then to his astonishment, Alexis noticed something else: The blanket covering Marie Ferrand's distended abdomen was gradually flattening out. "Look at her abdomen!" he cried, unable to contain his excitement. "The bell of the basilica had just struck three . . . minutes later, there was no longer any sign of distention in Marie Ferrand's abdomen," he wrote. Even as Alexis watched and continued recording his notes, he felt that he was losing his senses; what he was seeing was impossible. Marie Ferrand's breathing normalized, and her heartbeat became regular.

"How do you feel?" he asked her.

"I feel very well," she answered. "I am still weak, but I feel I am cured."

Alexis wrote:

There was no longer any doubt. Marie Ferrand's condition was improving so much that she was scarcely recognizable. . . . In a few minutes she raised her head, looked around, moved her limbs a little, then turned over on her side, without having shown the least sign of pain. . . . A dying girl is recovering!

Alexis went to report the event to Dr. Boissarie, chief doctor of the Lourdes clinic. After listening to his colleague describe what had transpired, Dr. Boissarie said, "This inexplicable power in Lourdes has cured cancers, tumors, and even tuberculosis. We have seen it many times and must concede it. This is not the first time that a tubercular peritonitis has disappeared. I have several records of it in my office." He then recounted several dramatic cases of other dying patients healed at the grotto.

When Marie Ferrand was returned to the hospital, Alexis performed a thorough examination; the hard masses in her abdomen had vanished. Except for the weakness generated by her prolonged illness, and her still-swollen legs, she seemed completely normal. She was cured. Two other doctors also examined her and reached the same conclusion.

This healing that occurred before his eyes caused a crisis in Dr. Alexis Carrel's soul. He tried by every means to discount it, yet none of his arguments held up against the evidence of his own experience and scientific investigation. He knew of other doctors who had gone to Lourdes who were so disturbed by the evidence of mysterious healings that they refused to admit having been there. Now he understood their dilemma.

Long into the night, Alexis paced up and down by the grotto, wrestling with a spiritual dilemma that had become intensely personal. If he reported what he'd seen and had verified, he risked ridicule — the loss of prestige and respect among his colleagues.

Yet if he denied or withheld the truth, as he was tempted to do, he risked losing both his integrity and self-respect.

Through a sleepless night, Dr. Carrel weighed his career against his soul. As dawn approached, he began to pray for the first time in many years. As he did, something inside him was reconciled, resolved, and healed.

The incident at Lourdes was a turning point in the life and career of Dr. Alexis Carrel. In the following years he spent much time researching and investigating the phenomenon of miraculous healings. His thorough report, when it was finally written and published, included the fruits of these years of research, as well as an account of the event at Lourdes that had changed the course of his life. As he had feared, his report did result in controversy and public attacks on his character. Yet he courageously defended himself and his findings in the press.

Many years later, Dr. Alexis Carrel — by then a famed surgeon awarded the Nobel Prize for his medical research and discoveries — wrote:

> *We must liberate man from the cosmos created by the genius of physicists and astronomers, that cosmos in which, since the Renaissance, he has been imprisoned. We now know that we ...extend outside the physical continuum.... In time, as in space, the individual stretches out beyond the frontiers of his body.... He also belongs to another world.*

That other world, where the laws of known physics are transcended by laws yet unknown, was revealed to a skeptical young surgeon by the healing of Marie Ferrand in the grotto at Lourdes. But Marie was not the only person transformed that day. Her healing had become his own.

LOVE ON THE LINE

Saving Souls on the Streets

Before Christ spoke to Bill Tomes from a painting on the altar of St. Joseph's Church, he'd lived a relatively ordinary, if somewhat adventurous life. A middle-class boy from Evanston, Illinois, and a talented painter with a love of football, Bill attended Notre Dame and earned a bachelor's degree in English and philosophy, and a master's degree in counseling and guidance. He lived fully, pursued his art, dated, and drank with his friends. He traveled throughout Europe (nine trips) visiting twenty-eight nations, collecting antiques, and interviewing various psychiatrists as preparation for his doctoral dissertation.

Then in 1980 a simple dilemma took him to the altar of St. Joseph's Church in Chicago. He'd been offered two very different, well-paying jobs: one as a hospital therapist and the other a promising position with a major airline.

"When I knelt down, hoping for guidance," Bill explained, "everything turned dark and fuzzy except the face of Christ on a painting near the altar."

Then a voice that Bill believed was that of Christ commanded him: "Love," it said. "You are forbidden to do anything other than that."

Bill, not a particularly religious man, was astonished. The life he'd led the past forty-five years had not prepared him for such an event. Next, his prayer over which job to take was answered: The same voice said three times: "I'll lead, you follow." And then, "Never be afraid." And five times in a row, "All your trust."

Bewildered, yet struck to the core, Bill revisited the altar and the painting numerous times over the next few months. Later, in another location, Christ continued to utter direct commandments, instructing him with the following words: "You must forgive everyone everything." And, "Judge not, and you will not be judged."

Several months passed. Bill struggled to understand the meaning of his experience as well as these commandments — to know how to carry them out. He started reading the Bible and other religious books. At one point he encountered the line "Take nothing with you for the journey" seven times in a row in three books, until it became personally significant. After prolonged resistance to the apparent implications, and with the intervention of a priest, Bill gave in — and gave away nearly every possession he had. Keeping only his clothes, he moved into a friend's basement, where he slept on cardboard, and began working manual labor, for food only — not accepting money.

Bill had worked until 1978 as a counselor for Catholic Charities, a community service organization. Then, after going into art and other work, in 1983 he was offered, and accepted, a position as a youth minister working with street gangs in the Chicago projects. His first visit there was greeted with everything from indifference to hurled objects. He viewed the challenge of these youths as a test of his commitment. After Bill's next visit, he later learned, one local gang met to consider whether or not he should be killed. They decided he was a good guy and that he should be allowed to do what he thought he should, and that he would be "protected," which meant they planned to kill anyone who dared to hurt him. Bill spoke against this kind of protection.

Little by little Bill got to know the troubled gang members, and their territory became his own. At Cardinal Bernardin's request, Bill's ministry grew in time to include other gang-infested projects. Others joined Bill, and he found himself with a large, troubled flock of at-risk youth, outsiders, and outcasts, most of them living on the edge of death, many fated to be casualties of the code of violence that lay at the center of their lives.

Brother Bill, as he came to be called, has personally encountered that violence, often in tragic forms — like the time he found a young gang leader dying in a stairwell with four bullets in his chest. All a grief-stricken Brother Bill could think to do was to hold the twenty-one-year-old man and whisper in his ear, "God made you. He loves you. He wants you to be with him forever." Perhaps it was enough.

This incident was one of many that demonstrated the earnestness and commitment that Bill Tomes brought to life in carrying out Christ's personal commandment to "love without judgment" over many years.

Brother Bill didn't always feel loving, but he always did his best to show love in tangible ways, in action. He treated all he met with all the kindness and compassion he could bring to bear. He showed love to seemingly unlovable souls by spending time with them, playing basketball, taking them to football games, helping them find work if they wanted it — by countless, simple acts of kindness and generosity offered with no strings attached. Brother Bill understood that these young men found deeds more powerful than words, and that acting with simple kindness was more potent than preaching. So he didn't preach; his was a ministry of love, support, and the faith that a power many call God would somehow penetrate the hearts and minds of the souls in his care.

Ron Stodghill wrote of Brother Bill in a *Time* magazine article:

> *He believes that gangsters will not change their ways simply through fear of prison or even the carrot of education or employment . . . but only by viewing themselves as under the light of a divine presence. . . . His vulnerability, his willingness to put his life on the line, his unconditional offering of acceptance and forgiveness, and yes, love, are a constant source of astonishment for men and boys weaned on hate and rejection.*
>
> *"I think he's an angel," says a twenty-two-year-old Vice Lord. "I really think God sent him here."*

But Brother Bill has shown his love and proven the courage of his convictions by following another of Christ's injunctions: "No greater love can a man show, than that he be willing to lay down his life for his friends."

Dozens and dozens of times over the years, Bill Tomes walked into the line of fire and stood between two warring gangs until they stopped shooting. They did stop, sometimes reluctantly. He was often secretly told by gang members what was "coming down." His sources probably ranged from a reluctant tough ordered to make a hit on an opposing gang member, to a boy who didn't want to engage in a shooting skirmish but couldn't back out in front of his friends. Whatever the reason, they called Brother Bill. And he came — often after the shooting had already begun. He walked out and stood in the midst of the flying bullets. When they shouted at him to get out of the way, he told them he wouldn't, because he loved them. They could see it in his eyes, in his posture, and in his commitment by being there. Is there greater proof of love than this? Maybe that's why they stopped shooting.

Over 150 of Brother Bill's "parishioners" have died over the years — from drugs, beatings, knives, and bullets — some of them innocent bystanders, who by living in these neighborhoods also live in the line of fire. One woman criticized Brother Bill for giving too much of himself to those who were bringing so much pain and trouble to the neighborhoods. While he understood her point of view, he explained that he was called to follow higher instructions. Gang leaders have said that five hundred lives have been saved — saved through the extraordinary efforts of Bill Tomes, working tirelessly for peace on the streets.

Jesus Christ, who also lived among outcasts, and who said, "I have come to call not the saved, but the sinners, to righteousness," has served as Bill Tomes's role model and inspiration — his commander on a spiritual battlefield where real lives are on the line, real bullets are fired, and real blood spilled. And so Brother Bill has ministered to his flock of prodigal sons, calling them home through love.

A SLEEPING GIFT AWAKENS

The Revelations of a Modest Prophet

Edgar Cayce was born in 1877 on a Kentucky farm to devout but uneducated parents. He himself would not pass beyond the ninth grade. A quiet, deeply religious boy, he was also a bit otherworldly; until he was nine years old, "little folk" that only he and his friend Anna could see came out of the woods to play with them. One little fellow once told them, "We live in the flowers and the music."

"What music?" Anna had asked.

"The music of everything," the little fellow replied.

Anna died that winter. In the spring, a lonely Edgar looked for her in the flowers with the little folk. But he never found her.

At age ten, Edgar made a vow to read the Bible once through for every year of his life. Over the next three years he read the Bible thirteen times. One day while studying his Bible in a secret place in the woods, he felt a presence near him. He looked up and saw a beautiful woman with shadowy appendages on her back shaped like wings. Her voice, when she spoke, was soft and musical: "Your prayers have been heard," she told Edgar. "Tell me what you would like most of all so that I may give it to you."

After hesitating, Edgar mustered his courage and said, "Most of all I would like to be helpful to others, and especially to children when they are sick."

As suddenly as she had come, the woman vanished.

All the next day, Edgar's mind was dull. His teacher reported his poor school performance to his father, a stern man everyone called Squire. Disgraced, Squire tested Edgar on his schoolbooks that night, and in frustration at his son's seeming stupidity, he slapped Edgar and knocked him to the floor. That's when Edgar heard her voice: "If you sleep a little, we can help you," the angel said.

Edgar pleaded with his father for a chance to rest. He promised he would know the lesson when he woke. After his father went into the kitchen, Edgar curled up on his chair with his schoolbook under his head, and fell fast asleep.

When the Squire woke Edgar minutes later to test him, he was astonished to find that Edgar could now answer any question on any page of the book, much of which he hadn't even read. After that, Edgar slept with his schoolbooks under his pillow, and in the morning he would know their entire contents — he saw the pages in his mind. He was soon moved a grade ahead in school.

Two years later, after a baseball struck Edgar on the spine, he came home delirious and acting strangely. When his worried parents put him to bed, he fell asleep and began to speak. In a calm, clear voice he told his parents of his spinal injury and described in detail how to make a poultice that would cure him. They followed his instructions, and by morning his symptoms were gone and his spine healed. Edgar had no memory of the previous day or of his sleeping diagnosis.

Years passed. Edgar grew up, left the farm, and moved to a

nearby town. He worked in a bookstore, where he met Gertrude, his future wife; they would eventually have three sons. Edgar became a photographer and a respected member of his church and community. He seemed in all ways ordinary, except for his secret talents, which manifested periodically.

A turning point came when Edgar healed himself of a serious throat condition using self-hypnosis, with the help of an amateur hypnotist named Lane. Lane began experimenting on Edgar. He found that when Edgar was in a trance he was able to diagnose others with uncanny accuracy, even when they were far away. Edgar had no medical background; yet in his trances he used precise medical terminology he didn't know when awake, and prescribed wide-ranging remedies that proved remarkably effective.

This young man was apparently a gifted doctor in his sleep.

Edgar was leery of his odd ability, and only after much persuasion by Lane and soul-searching on his own did he agree to use it. When he saw that the people who came to him were cured, he couldn't refuse. But he wouldn't accept any money. If his healing capacity was God's gift — and he prayed that it was — he could not in good conscience profit by it.

Edgar's medical advice was often vigorously opposed by doctors. They insisted his unorthodox treatments would prove disastrous and perhaps fatal to patients they themselves had been unable to help. At times, fearing the worst, Edgar suffered agonies of doubt. He knew that if one patient died it would ruin him. But seeing so many people healed gave him faith in his gift and the courage to use it.

Some of the doctors who first accused Edgar of quackery were won over by his remarkable cures and offered to team up with him, hoping to make their careers and fortunes. Edgar always declined.

To one such adversary-turned-entrepreneur he said, "You found that I'm not a fake like all the other doctors who investigated me. Now if you fellas could convince me that you all are not all fakes, maybe I'd join up with you."

When a nationally syndicated newspaper article appeared about this country boy with the miraculous gift, a flood of people came — believers seeking magical healing, hucksters seeking to exploit him for a buck, and skeptics seeking to expose him as a fraud. And thousands of desperate letters began pouring in, all requesting help. Often in trance Edgar gave detailed readings in answer, sometimes to letters that had not yet arrived.

Edgar Cayce would become known as the Sleeping Prophet. Arrested more than once — charged with fraud, fortune-telling, and practicing medicine without a license — he was always exonerated in the end. Not one person he diagnosed ever complained, and no one who followed his treatments ever died as a result. Cayce's percentage of documented cures was higher than those of the physicians of his time, or for that matter, of ours.

One day a man whose passion was metaphysics came to Edgar for a reading. When Edgar went into his trance, the man asked a wide range of metaphysical questions, and the readings took off into new territory. Edgar now spoke of reincarnation, karma, and of the *akashic records* — a library in another dimension where all knowledge and information was stored. These records, the reading said, were the source of the material given in Edgar's trances.

When Edgar woke and learned what he had said while asleep, he was unnerved, even frightened. The things he had spoken of while in trance, which he'd never read in his Bible, now turned his world upside down. He questioned his gift all over again. Did it come from God or from the devil? Was he possessed by demons?

How could he tell? He suffered a crisis of conscience, fearing a threat to his most cherished religious beliefs. After much thought and prayer he decided to apply biblical wisdom to the matter of his gift. By its fruits he would know it: He would examine the results of his readings in people's lives. If they were truly helped, then his special abilities must be God's gift. In that case, to withhold his readings would be the sin.

One day Edgar's son Hugh lit a pile of flash powder on the floor and it blew up in his face, burning both his eyes. Doctors told Edgar one eye would have to be removed to save his son's life. The other eye would likely remain blind. But young Hugh told the doctors his father could heal him. "When my daddy goes to sleep he's the best doctor in the world," he said. Then he asked his father to help him. In trance, Edgar prescribed a poultice using tannic acid to be placed on Hugh's burned eyes. The doctors opposed it. But as Hugh was already blind, the matter was academic. The poultice was applied. Hugh regained his sight.

Over the years Edgar's readings helped thousands of people, healing their bodies and renewing their faith. The readings always turned people to the purpose of existence — relationship with others and with God. Edgar was leery of metaphysical enthusiasts — those who dabbled in psychic phenomena for the sake of thrills or the aggrandizement of their egos. He feared such people would turn his work into a cult, and he wanted no part of it.

Edgar's mind was tuned to the cosmos, but his feet were now planted firmly on earth. He knew his knowledge must help people in tangible ways or it was of little value. Fascinating information was never the point. As the readings often said, "To know, and not to do, becomes sin." Truth, to be of value, had to be lived, not merely believed.

Over the years a vast body of medical and metaphysical wisdom came through Edgar's trances, emerging from the depths of some Universal Mind to which he seemed to be a conduit or bridge. He accurately prophesied many future events, including the Civil Rights movement and the assassinations of the Kennedy brothers and Martin Luther King, Jr. He foretold a spiritual renaissance, now occurring, in the last quarter of the twentieth century and the beginning of the twenty-first. Meanwhile he read his Bible daily, each year completing one cycle and keeping his childhood vow.

In 1943 Thomas Sugrue's biography of Edgar Cayce, *There Is a River*, was published. It resulted in an avalanche of letters from people requesting help. To meet the demand, Edgar tripled his daily readings. But the strain of it was too much, and his health began a rapid decline. His friends and family warned him to cut back and take it easy. But moved by the suffering of those who wrote to him for help, he could not turn away. In trance, Edgar even warned himself to rest immediately. When asked "How long shall Edgar rest?" the Sleeping Prophet answered in the third person: "Until he is well or dead." A prophet to the end.

Edgar Cayce died on January 3, 1945. His last words were, "How much the world needs God today." Three months later, on Easter Sunday, his wife Gertrude followed him. An extraordinary life had run its course after enriching the lives of many others. In his lifetime Edgar directly helped more than thirty thousand people. His readings, all recorded, now reside in the Association for Research and Enlightenment in Virginia Beach, Virginia.

The life of Edgar Cayce points to a fairy-tale reality where winged angels grant prayers in lonely woods to humble youths, where little people teach children about "the music of everything,"

and where simple souls grow up to help heal the world with their
magical gifts. But more important, Edgar's life and work remind
us that the world in which we live is more mysterious than we
know, and that spiritual powers lie dormant within each of us,
waiting to be awakened and used in the service of others.

EPILOGUE

Opening the Mind to Mystery

Take courage;
the human race is divine.

— PYTHAGORAS

Nowhere do we find a more perfect field of debate between believers and skeptics than in the area of UFO research, where interested parties range from outright frauds and pranksters, to wild-eyed conspiracy theorists, to the most diligent scientific investigators. Whether discussing unidentified flying objects or healing powers, shamanic visits to the underworld, ghostly visitations, or visitors from other star systems, we each confront the fundamental question "What is true?" Despite modern technology and the scientific method, this question has never been an easy one to answer with certainty.

In the late 1950s a young French astrophysicist, Dr. Jacques Vallée, began working in an observatory outside Paris. There he observed two remarkable phenomena: First, from time to time unidentified objects appeared on the radar screen, maneuvering in ways far beyond the capacity of known human technology, performing seemingly impossible feats. Moving at speeds in the thousands of miles per hour, they made right-angle turns, instantaneous stops, and even reversed direction all without slowing down — impossible maneuvers by our current technological standards.

Second, Vallée's colleagues and superiors, elite scientists at the top of their profession, routinely destroyed the records showing what these unidentified objects were capable of doing. When Vallée asked them why, they told him that to report these anomalous events would only cause trouble and might even jeopardize their careers.

Vallée had become a scientist to learn the nature of reality and discover the truths of the universe. Now he was a witness to, and passive participant in, both the discovery and the cover-up of extraordinary phenomena, perhaps of historic significance. Young Dr. Vallée weighed his scientific career against his scientific integrity.

In the end, the compelling nature and significance of the phenomena and denial by his colleagues would change the course of Vallée's life and work. Knowing he wouldn't be able to investigate such phenomena in his current position, he quit his job and began traveling around the world as a full-time UFO investigator. He also studied records of other extraordinary (and possibly related) phenomena from various cultures and historical eras, which included reports of similar UFO sightings, as well as of angels, ghosts, spirits, and other supposedly supernatural apparitions.

Vallée ran these reports through a custom computer program and found that these seemingly diverse phenomena shared uncanny parallels with twentieth-century UFO sightings. In other words, similar or parallel phenomena had occurred in nearly every culture in every age. And taken as a whole, these phenomena appeared to be phases of a continuous event of contact, whether with other worlds or with other dimensions of reality — or with unknown dimensions of the human psyche — reported in language and within the belief structures of the age in which they appeared.

Vallée applied a rigorous scientific process of observing facts while avoiding beliefs and emotional or ideological attachment to any particular outcome. After years of investigation, he remained an objective scientist. Neither believing nor disbelieving, he has gathered evidence and drawn working hypotheses and a tentative conclusion based on his research: From earliest times to the present, humanity has been visited by apparently intelligent entities who have appeared in various guises, yet whose nature and origins remain a mystery.

By 1979 Dr. Vallée, after having investigated tens of thousands of reported UFO sightings, compiled a list of two thousand documented, unexplained "close encounters" from around the world over a twenty-year period. After two decades of exhaustive research, he proposed that UFO phenomena, like reports of extraordinary experiences involving spirits and other nonhuman entities, might not be entirely random events.

UFOs, the latest and most modern form of mysterious apparitions, are a verifiable phenomenon; the term *UFO* as used here doesn't refer to so-called flying saucers or "little green men," but to a small but significant percentage of reliable, credible, and well-investigated eyewitness reports that haven't yet been, and perhaps cannot be, explained or debunked. They appear in the skies surrounding the globe. They show up on radar in observatories around the world. They are captured on film and leave marks on the earth, and even on human bodies. And it is possible that in the coming years, perhaps soon, such extraordinary experiences will become part of the fabric of our everyday lives, reshaping our cultures and our world.

As the spiritual savant Emanuel Swedenborg and the pioneering psychiatrist Carl Jung suggested before him, Dr. Jacques Vallée has suggested that spiritual, supernatural, and extraterrestrial entities and phenomena may originate in some part of the human psyche itself, while in many cases also maintaining their own independent existence. And such sightings or encounters are an intentional, interactive phenomenon: They appear in forms that respond to our needs, hopes, and expectations, even as they shape our beliefs, our myths, our lives, our world, and no doubt our future.

In *Dimensions*, his summary book on the subject, Vallée wrote:

> *Our brains erect a ladder of symbols toward the darkened skies where the strange machines hover, and we meet them more than halfway across the bridge of their strangeness — perhaps because we vaguely perceive that their adventure is closely related to our own. But the extraterrestrial theory is not good enough, because it is not strange enough to explain the facts.*

We believe the stories in this book suggest compelling evidence of very real phenomena, and a pattern of contact similar to that identified by Jacques Vallée, Carl Jung, Emanuel Swedenborg, and others. Throughout human history, people of every faith, and of no faith at all, have reported extraordinary experiences and events that have awakened remarkable abilities and gifts, and transformed lives, communities, and even entire cultures. Today's high-tech entities, allegedly from extraterrestrial worlds or other dimensions, are but the latest guests in a historical list of mythic others intervening in our world.

While some look to the skies for hope or personal salvation, or

perhaps for a preview of our collective human potential, others look inward, seeking in the depths of our consciousness the archetypal keys to our past, future, and purpose here. This journey into inner space may be the greatest adventure of all. And as both astral and etheric phenomena increasingly emerge into the light of modern-day awareness, veils between worlds continue to part, revealing newfound wisdom and perspective, transforming lives, catalyzing life missions, and reinventing our global culture.

Perhaps that bridge between worlds — between earth and heaven, between the seemingly mundane world we take for granted and that mystical place where matter, energy, and spirit merge — lies within each of us, ready to awaken us to a higher consciousness and a greater vision of reality.

Whatever the ultimate nature of mysterious sightings, miraculous healings, and extraordinary revelations that change the course of lives, we had best try to understand them, to grasp their meaning and purpose. For they are even now touching the lives of millions worldwide, shifting our modern spiritual landscape, and shaping our visions of tomorrow.

ACKNOWLEDGMENTS

O ur gratitude to all those who helped, directly or indirectly, in the creation of this book. Thanks to Linda Kramer of H J Kramer Inc. and Jason Gardner, senior editor at New World Library, whose graceful collaboration and clear literary instincts helped shape this revised and much improved book. Heartfelt thanks also to our literary agent, Candice Fuhrman, for her instincts, integrity, objectivity, and support in ways both numerous and ongoing.

Thanks also to freelance editor and word sculptor Nancy Carleton, whose consistently discerning and insightful eyes helped to shape, polish, and refine our writing efforts.

We are also indebted to researchers, biographers, and others whose germinal work formed a foundation and starting point for our inquiries into the realm of extraordinary phenomena — people such as Dr. Jacques Vallée, PhD, astrophysicist, researcher, and author viewed by many as the real-life model for the French scientist in *Close Encounters of the Third Kind*.

Many thanks, too, to each and every contributor who personally submitted, related, and permitted us to use their stories: Carol Benjamin, George Esteban (Si Tai Gong), Don "Four Arrows" Jacobs, Allison James, Sean Kilcoyne, Andy Lakey, Patrice Somé Malidoma, Richard Sabinski, Jack and Lois Schwarz, Ed Spielman, Nancy Siscoe, Brother Bill Tomes, and Valerie Vener.

Special appreciation to the following manuscript readers willing to sample our cake before it was fully baked, and to offer their recipe suggestions: Reneé Brewer, Brenda Brown, Holly Demé, Elsa Dixon, Barry Elkin, Candice Fuhrman, Dawn Michelle Glanzman, Karen Pierce González, Isa Howard-Cohen, Allison James, Dave Kraft, Chuck Marco, Julia Marrero, Christine McDermott, Joy Millman, David Moyer, Sandra Nadalin, Dwight and Celeste Parcel, Terry Patton, Heather (and Madeleine) Picard, Sharon Root, and Beth Wilson.

APPENDIX

Literary Sources and Resources

The stories you've read in this volume emerged from a global heritage of cultures and epochs. The authors spoke personally with only a handful of the principals involved. In many cases, we were limited to searching and researching well-documented literary sources. Most often, we found two or more sources to serve as cross-references and background for historical accuracy. We're grateful to the authors of the following sources, who provided the background — and the shoulders on which we stood — to relate, in our own words, extraordinary experiences that transformed lives.

Anonymous. *Alcoholics Anonymous*. New York: Alcoholics Anonymous World Services, 1976.
————. *Pass It On: The Story of Bill Wilson and How the A.A. Message Reached the World*. New York: Alcoholics Anonymous World Services Inc., 1984.
Atwater, P.M.H. *Beyond the Light: What Isn't Being Said about the Near-Death Experience*. New York: Carol Publishing Group, 1994.
————. *Future Memory*. Charlottesville, VA: Hampton Roads, 1999.
Basham, A. L. *The Wonder That Was India*. New York: Taplinger Publishing, 1967.
Carrel, Alexis. *The Voyage to Lourdes*. New York: Harper Brothers, 1950.
Carty, Charles Mortimer. *Padre Pio: The Stigmatist*. Rockford, IL: Tan Books, 1989.
David-Neel, Alexandra. *Magic and Mystery in Tibet*. New York: Claude Kendall, 1932.
Durham, Michael S. *Miracles of Mary*. San Francisco: HarperCollins, 1995.
Green, Arthur, & Holtz, Barry. *Your Word Is Fire: The Hasidic Masters on Contemplative Prayer*. Woodstock, VT: Jewish Lights Publishing, 1993.
Hatch, Alden. *Buckminster Fuller: At Home in the Universe*. New York: Crown, 1974.

Jacobs, Don Trent. *Primal Awareness*. Rochester, NY: Inner Traditions, 1998.

James, William. *The Varieties of Religious Experience*. New York: Collier-Macmillan, 1961.

Johnston, Francis. *The Wonder of Guadalupe*. Rockford, IL: Tan Books, 1981.

Jung, Carl. *Memories, Dreams, Reflections*. New York: Vintage Books, 1965.

Kaplan, Justin. *Walt Whitman: A Life*. New York: Simon & Schuster, 1980.

Kapleau, Philip. *The Three Pillars of Zen*. Boston: Beacon Press, 1965.

Kasich, John. *Courage Is Contagious*. New York: Doubleday, 1998.

Ke Yun Lu. "New Century," published in *October Magazine*, Beijing, China, 1991.

Monroe, Robert A. *Journeys Out of the Body*. New York: Anchor Doubleday, 1977.

———. *Far Journeys*. New York: Doubleday Books, 1985.

Morse, Melvin, & Perry, Paul. *Transformed by the Light*. New York: Villard Books, 1997.

Peace Pilgrim. *Peace Pilgrim: Her Life and Work in Her Own Words*. Santa Fe: Ocean Tree Books, 1994.

Ronner, John. *The Angels of Cokeville and Other True Stories of Heavenly Intervention*. Murfreesboro, TN: Mamre Press, 1995.

Rossman, Doreen Mary. *A Light Shone in the Darkness: The Story of Stigmatist and Mystic Therese Neumann*. Santa Barbara, CA: Queenship Publishing, 1997.

Schulberg, Lucille. *Historic India: Great Ages of Man*. New York: Time-Life Books, 1968.

Spear, Percival. *India*. Ann Arbor: University of Michigan Press, 1961.

Spielman, Ed. *The Spiritual Journey of Joseph L. Greenstein: The Mighty Atom*. New York: First Glance Books, 1998.

Steiger, Brad. *Revelation: The Divine Fire*. New Jersey: Prentice Hall, 1973.

Sugrue, Thomas. *There Is a River: The Story of Edgar Cayce*. New York: Dell Books, 1967.

Terrell, John Upton. *Journey into Darkness: A True Account of Cabeza De Vaca's Remarkable Expedition across the North American Continent*. New York: William Morrow, 1962.

Underhill, Evelyn. *Mysticism*. New York: Dutton Books, 1961.

Vallée, Jacques. *Passport to Magonia*. Chicago: Contemporary Books, 1969.

van der Post, Laurens. *About Blady*. New York: William Morrow, 1991.

Van Dusen, Wilson. *The Presence of Other Worlds*. New York: Swedenborg Foundation, 1974.

Wakefield, Dan. *Expect a Miracle*. San Francisco: HarperCollins, 1995.

Walsh, William Thomas. *Our Lady of Fatima*. New York: Image Books, Doubleday, 1990.

Weber, Christin Lore. *A Cry in the Desert: The Awakening of Byron Katie*. Barstow, CA: The Work Foundation, 1996.

INDEX OF PEOPLE

Well-Known, Historic, or Public Figures in This Book

ABOUT DAN MILLMAN

D an Millman, a former world-champion athlete and college professor, is the author of numerous books, including *Way of the Peaceful Warrior*, *Wisdom of the Peaceful Warrior*, *The Life You Were Born to Live*, *The Laws of Spirit*, and *The Journeys of Socrates*. His writings have inspired millions of readers in more than thirty languages.

Dan teaches worldwide, sharing realistic ways to live with a peaceful heart and warrior spirit, transforming everyday life into a path of personal and spiritual growth. His work has influenced men and women from all walks of life, including leaders in the fields of health, psychology, education, business, politics, entertainment, sports, and the arts.

Dan and his family reside in Northern California.

For information about Dan Millman's books and seminars,
you are invited to visit his website:
www.peacefulwarrior.com

ABOUT DOUG CHILDERS

Doug Childers has coauthored four published books: the critically acclaimed *The White-Haired Girl* (St. Martin's/Picador) with Jaia Sun (an Alternate Selection of the Book-of-the-Month Club); *The Energy Prescription* (Bantam/Random House) with Connie Grauds; *Minding Your Business* (Mandala Press) with Horst Rechelbacher (winner of the Nautilus Gold Award for Conscious Leadership in Business) and *Bridge Between Worlds* (H J Kramer/New World Library) with Dan Millman. A professional ghostwriter, freelance editor, and book doctor for nearly twenty years, Doug has worked on hundreds of books in the fields of psychology/spirituality, memoirs, body/mind medicine, and fiction.

Doug lives in Northern California, where he devotes his time to his own works in progress.

For information about the literary works and
editorial/collaborative services of Doug Childers,
you are invited to visit his website:
www.dougchilders.com

H J Kramer and New World Library are dedicated to
publishing books and audio products that inspire
and challenge us to improve the quality
of our lives and our world.

Our products are available
in bookstores everywhere.
For our catalog, please contact:

H J Kramer / New World Library
14 Pamaron Way
Novato, California 94949

Phone: (415) 884-2100 or (800) 972-6657
Catalog requests: Ext. 50
Orders: Ext. 52
Fax: (415) 884-2199

E-mail: escort@newworldlibrary.com
Website: www.newworldlibrary.com